INTERNATIONAL ECONOMIC PROBLEMS

International Economic Problems

LEONARD GOMES

ST. MARTIN'S PRESS NEW YORK

© Leonard Gomes 1978

All rights reserved. For information, write:
St. Martin's Press, Inc., 175 Fifth Avenue, New York, N.Y. 10010
Printed in Great Britain
First published in the United States of America in 1979
ISBN 0–312–42158–3

Library of Congress Cataloguing in Publication Data

Gomes, Leonard.
   International economic problems.

   Includes bibliographical references and index.
   1. International economic relations.   I.   Title.
HF1411.G653   1979   382.1   78–12769
ISBN 0–312–42158–3

Contents

List of Tables

Preface

This book was designed to meet the need for a policy or problem-orientated text to complement an introductory theory text in the field of international economics. General texts, more often than not, treat international policy issues in a rather cursory fashion. This book remedies this deficiency by offering the student and the general reader an up-to-date, comprehensive and critical analysis of the keenly debated issues in international economic relations. Its purpose is to bridge the gap between the abstractions of economic theory and the complexity of economic decision-making and policy. By providing concise statements of the major problems confronting the world economy it serves as a source of topics for essays or project work assigned to students who have mastered the basic theory.

A theme that runs throughout the book is the clash of national interests against the constraints imposed on national policy-making by the inexorable trend towards interdependence in the world economy. This problem is specifically treated in the Introduction, but its undertones can be discerned in subsequent chapters. Chapter 1 discusses the issues involved in the current Tokyo Round of multilateral trade negotiations. This is followed by chapters on the trade problems of the Third World and an analysis of the new frontiers in East—West trade. The integration of money markets across the Atlantic and, indeed, financial integration in the wider world is the subject of Chapter 4, which examines the role of the Eurodollar market in this development. Chapter 5 looks at the problems of the international monetary system and discusses the failures and achievements of the post-war IMF system established at Bretton Woods — a system designed to institutionalise monetary co-operation as a permanent feature of international economic relations. Nowhere (apart from the area of commercial policy) is the tension between international interdependence and national sovereignty more acute than in the sphere of international monetary arrangements. The conflicts that brought down the Bretton Woods system are described, as are the attempts to rebuild a new monetary order. The impact of multinational corporations on the world economy is the topic of Chapter 6. The book ends with a survey of recent empirical and theoretical explanations of the pattern of international trade in manufactured goods. An understanding of the underlying forces in trade patterns is appropriate in the context of the trade liberalisation and adjustment measures now currently being discussed in the Tokyo Round.

In all the discussions the findings of the very latest research are incorporated.

Throughout the text references to 'billion' = United States billion, i.e. 1 thousand million.

LEONARD GOMES

Acknowledgements

The author and publishers wish to thank the following organisations who have kindly co-operated in granting permission to quote tabular matter published by them:

The Bank for International Settlements, Basle.
General Agreement on Tariffs and Trade, Geneva.
The International Monetary Fund, Washington, D.C.
The Ministry of International Trade and Industry, Japanese Government.
The Morgan Guaranty Trust Company of New York.
The United Nations.
The United Nations Conference on Trade and Development.

Every effort has been made to trace all copyright-holders, but if any have been inadvertently overlooked the publishers will be pleased to make the necessary arrangement at the first opportunity.

Introduction

Since the end of the last war economists have pointed to the fact of growing interdependence among countries in the world economy; but it was only in the early 1970s that the reality of interdependence was brought home to national policy-makers. The breakdown of the Bretton Woods monetary system in 1971 and the commodity crisis of 1973–4 were the dramatic turn of events which produced the new awareness of mutual dependency.

These shocks to the world economy exposed the vulnerability of national economies and, in particular, their capacity to provide ever-increasing standards of well-being for their citizens on the basis of given resource endowments and traditional patterns of trade and investment. In the 1973–4 commodity boom the prices of raw materials and industrial commodities from copper to scrap steel, to oil and rubber reached unprecedented heights. Although in 1975 most prices, with the exception of oil and some foods, fell almost as dramatically as they had risen, they remained above pre – 1972 levels. The shortage mentality this engendered jolted the industrial countries, including the United States, into a heightened state of awareness of their dependence on foreign supply. The commodity crisis seemed to confirm the gloomy forecasts of the 'eco-doomsters' that the world was running out of resources. Fears were expressed that in a world of increasing scarcity natural resource owners would be able to extract growing rents and that bargaining power in commodity markets was irrevocably shifting towards the sellers.

At the same time the less developed countries in UNCTAD, inspired to new militancy by the success of OPEC, pressed for a 'new international economic order' of which the main elements were a better deal in commodity trade and larger resource transfers from the rich countries. The developed countries, for their part, found themselves in the deepest recession since before the war combined with historically high rates of inflation. Faced with common problems, both in relation to the management of their own economies as well as in connection with the appropriate response to the demands of the LDCs, leaders of industrial countries began to talk of 'interdependence' as the only sensible principle for the conduct of international relations. For instance, this was the theme at the May 1977 economic summit of seven Western countries. The Western leaders stressed the dangers of protectionism and the need to find joint solutions to the common problems of unemployment, inflation, oil debts, energy and the trade problems of the Third World. As regards relations with the Third World the negotiating stance of the rich countries is decidedly more conciliatory.

The participation of the industrial countries in the Conference on International Economic Co-operation – the North–South Dialogue – expresses the new attitude of mutual dependence. Launched in December 1975, the Conference which includes OPEC countries and representatives of the LDCs seeks to reach broad agreement on the issues involved in the new international economic order. The participation of the major oil-producing countries in the continuing North–South dialogue is a recognition of their increased importance in international economic relations. By the same token, the power they wield can be used to extract concessions from the rich countries favourable to Third World countries. Leaders in some developed countries have come to see their own self-interest as intimately bound up with the economic fortunes of the poor countries. Apart from the fear that Third World frictions with the slow pace of economic development can lead to political instability the feeling is growing that the most effective way out of world recession and unemployment is to expand earnings in the Third World through a programme of resource transfers from the industrial countries.

In the last few years, therefore, nations have been behaving as if they accept the dictates of an interdependent world economy. This expresses itself in greater efforts at international co-operation on major issues. Whether this new awareness is merely temporary is anybody's guess. Certainly cynics can point to the revival of mercantilism and the broad appeal of purely national remedies for the ills of industrial society. In rough weather countries will opt for going it alone. But there can be no doubt that the contemporary international economic environment is one which imposes constraints (in some cases severe ones) on even the most self-sufficient country; and to the extent that international considerations are taken into account the effectiveness of national actions thereby increases.

How then is interdependence to be understood? There are obviously degrees of interdependence, and writers have identified three different uses of the notion: (*a*) a state of affairs where actions or policies of one country have a direct effect on economic circumstances in another country. This was said to be the relationship between Europe and the United States during the 1950s, euphemistically expressed in the saying: 'When America sneezes, Europe catches cold'; (*b*) interdependence implies increased national sensitivity to external economic developments, in the sense that changes in national economic variables, e.g. interest rates or money supply are constrained at values set by international factors; (*c*) a stringent definition put forward by Kenneth Waltz that interdependence entails 'a relationship that would be too costly to break'.[1]

On all three definitions, the judgement that economic interdependence among countries is high and increasing cannot be disputed. For the first time in the history of industrial society the term 'world economy' has acquired real meaning. The reduction of trade barriers, instant world-wide communications and global mobility have unified diverse economies to an extent undreamt of only fifty years ago. These developments, and other changes in the world economy, have led to a phenomenal expansion of world trade, a high degree of international financial integration and increased labour mobility. In the decade 1960–70 the volume of world trade increased by more than 8 per cent per annum and the trade of several industrial countries rose considerably faster. This rise in the share of world production moving across national boundaries poses rapid, sometimes painful, adjustment problems for national economies, but is another indicator of heightened interdependence within the international economy. The growing similarity of demand patterns has resulted in a broad similarity in the type and variety of export and import goods in the major trading countries. Multi-national firms have fostered a pattern of international production based on relative factor prices and resource endowments. Together with the spread of technology, the result has been to make national economies more similar in their basic characteristics of production. This uniformity in the technology of production is most marked among the industrial countries of North America and Western Europe. But in this area we are also witnessing an increasing trend towards a convergence of average labour costs in manufacturing industry. Labour mobility has increased, especially in Western Europe. International financial integration has accompanied economic integration. The degree of financial integration and international capital mobility – measured by the ratio of a country's commercial banks' foreign assets to the money supply – has increased among the industrial countries. This is reflected in the rapid growth of the Eurocurrency market since the mid-1960s.

Ironically, at the very time that the world economy has moved towards an interdependent system, economic nationalism has again become fashionable. Some commentators fear that the world is nearer sliding back into the protectionism of the 1930s than at any time for the last thirty years. Hopefully, responsible officials and politicians in Japan, the E.E.C. and the United States are fully alerted to the dangers. However, with all the industrial countries suffering from high unemployment, the pressure for import controls to protect existing jobs is difficult to withstand. Yet, there is no such thing as unilateral protection – a country seeing its products excluded from another's markets can, and will, retaliate with restrictive measures of its own. Besides, playing the protectionist game merely redistributes employment within a country with no net gain in jobs. For instance, import restrictions result in higher returns to import-competing industries. This allows such industries to expand and offer higher wages. But this, in turn, results in resources being bid away from other industries – including export industries.

The current wave of protectionism springs not only from the

misguided belief that import restrictions will increase national employment, but also reflects the general trend in the 1970s towards government intervention in private industry. To resist the pressures of increased interdependence of economies, national interests, both of labour and industry look to their national governments for relief and protection. Whether they are located in high-technology areas such as computers, or low-wage, declining industries such as textiles, management and labour tend to push governments along the protectionist road. The best hope, in the short run, of stemming the protectionist tide is speedy and tangible results in the current Tokyo Round of trade negotiations. This all major governments are pledged to achieve. In the long run, of course, much depends on a revival of the world economy and a general moderation of the rate of world inflation.

CHAPTER I

Multilateral Trade Negotiations

1.1 The Progress of Trade Liberalisation

One of the most heartening features of the post-war period has been the steady trend towards trade liberalisation, notably on the industrial tariff front. The momentum towards freer world trade was sustained in February 1975 when the seventh and most ambitious Round (known as the Tokyo Round) of international trade negotiations since 1947 started in Geneva under the auspices of GATT (the General Agreement on Tariffs and Trade). Formally launched in Tokyo in September 1973 as a follow-up to the Kennedy Round of tariff reductions of the 1960s the fate of the trade talks hung in the balance for over a year as the U.S. Congress withheld approval of the necessary legislation (President Nixon's Trade Bill) to provide the U.S. Administration with the authority to negotiate. Meanwhile the world economic situation had deteriorated – it became more sombre than at any time since the end of the last war, and certainly less favourable than the environment that accompanied the opening of the Kennedy Round in 1962. But the governments of the major trading countries were sufficiently alarmed at the prospect of a slide into protectionism[1] so that as soon as the U.S. Trade Reform Act was finally enacted early in 1975 no time was lost in proceeding with the substantive trade negotiations. The complex bargaining process involving about ninety countries is likely to take about two and a half years to complete. It would be many more years before the resulting agreement is ratified by national legislatures. The set of agreed rules would then apply for several decades, or into the next century.

The agenda of the Tokyo talks is a full one, comprising six

areas of negotiation: (i) the reduction or elimination of tariffs, (ii) liberalisation of non-tariff barriers to trade, (iii) examination of the multilateral safeguard system and particularly GATT Article 19 which authorises members to take emergency import-restricting measures if it can be shown that there is actual or threatened injury to domestic industries, (iv) liberalisation of trade in agricultural products, (v) special treatment of tropical products, and (vi) the feasibility of the 'sectoral approach' as a complementary liberalisation approach.

In the spirit of all previous GATT trade talks the negotiations are to be conducted on the basis of overall 'reciprocity' and 'non-discrimination'. Reciprocity ensures that the tariff reductions of each participant, called 'concessions', are at least roughly equal so that no country secures an apparent gain at the expense of its trading partners by giving up, overall, smaller concessions than it in turn receives from them. Obviously the products that enter the bargaining process are those in which both sides to a particular negotiation have an interest. But, by the second principle of non-discrimination, otherwise known as the 'most-favoured-nation clause' the bilaterally agreed liberalisation measures must be extended to all members not originally parties to the negotiation, except where the concessions form part of the creation of a common market. In this way a country's tariff remains uniform with respect to all other members of GATT, except again in the case of countries belonging to common markets or participating in preference schemes where two-column tariffs are maintained, the lower tariff being charged on imports from countries receiving preferential treatment and the higher, less favourable, rate being the MFN rate.

The issues to be resolved in the current negotiations must be seen against the background of the substantial progress made over the past quarter of a century (especially during the Kennedy Round) in dismantling the high tariff walls that had impeded the flow of world trade. The Kennedy Round resulted in across-the-board tariff cuts averaging more than 35 per cent on manufactured goods whose total trade value at that time amounted to $40,000m. The main industrial countries made tariff reductions covering 70 per cent of their dutiable imports

Table 1.1

Average Level of Customs Duties After the Kennedy Round (per cent)

	Raw materials	Semi-manufactures	Finished goods	Average
E.E.C.	0.7	7.7	9.2	7.0
United States	3.8	9.1	8.2	7.5
Japan	6.0	9.6	11.5	9.8

Source: *Analysis of Tariffs* (Geneva: GATT, 1971).

(excluding grains, meat and dairy products). Two-thirds of these cuts were of 50 per cent or more and about one-fifth were between 25–50 per cent. As a consequence, the average tariff level on imports of manufactures into the industrialized members of GATT fell from 10.9 to 6.2 per cent – Table 1.1 shows the average post-Kennedy-Round tariff levels for the major trading countries. These were typically products characterised by advanced technology or high capital intensity and only of marginal significance to the developing countries. Although a number of major concessions were made on some items of special importance to developing countries, the products in which these countries had expressed particular interest received on average smaller tariff reductions than other products. Tariff reductions were effected on only one-eighth of their total exports. Because the developing countries had little or nothing to offer by way of concessions to the developed countries, they were not parties to the major deals; they remained on the sidelines. Nevertheless they benefited from the bargains struck among the developed countries to the extent that their exports overlapped with products manufactured in the developed countries. In a sense they got something for nothing. But it was not nearly as good as it looked, because not being actively involved in the last negotiations, the developing countries own tariffs remain very high and their manufactured exports face highly restrictive barriers in the markets of the developed countries.

Although the Kennedy Round talks mounted a successful assault on *tariff* barriers, it was far less successful in tackling other equally important trade impediments, such as non-tariff barriers (NTBs) and agricultural protectionism. Indeed the talks almost foundered upon the inability of the major countries to settle on agriculture. Negotiators in the present talks hope to carry on where the last Round left off and do better this time in coming to grips with the intractable problems of NTBs and the liberalisation of trade in temperate food products (discussed in the following two sections). The negotiating countries will also be taking a hard, serious look at the principles and rules of conduct traditionally associated with GATT. Many believe that the provisions of GATT are in need of revision, restatement or modification in view of the serious inroads that have been made in them over the years. For instance, there has been a marked retreat from the principle of non-discrimination and reciprocity in response to pressures and the desire of countries to form preferential trading blocs. Thus the developed countries, under the terms of the 1966 Section 4 of GATT, no longer look for reciprocal concessions from the developing countries in trade negotiations. Likewise it is doubtful that MFN or non-discrimination is still the rule. This principle has been breached, first in favour of developing countries on the grounds that 'unequals should be treated unequally' (the approval of the Generalised System of Preferences for developing countries, GSP) and, second, as an exception, in order to allow the formation of regional customs unions or free-trade areas. In particular the E.E.C.'s policy of further extending the scope of its preferential arrangements to include Mediterranean, African and other countries has reinforced the cynical view that preferential treatment is now the rule and MFN the exception.

Article 19 – the safeguard clause of GATT – will also be scrutinised. It authorises a member country to impose emergency import quotas to stem a surge of imports that is causing or liable to cause 'material injury' to a domestic industry. This provision enjoins member countries contemplating such safeguard action to consult with the offending countries and to apply import restrictive measures in a non-discriminatory manner. However, this rule has remained a dead letter because countries managed to get round its provisions in practice by arranging for 'voluntary' export restraints to be exercised by the country whose exports were causing the alleged injury. Often the offending country's compliance with voluntary export quotas was secured under the veiled threat that unless they did so the importing country would adopt restrictions (i.e. retaliation) that might be even more severe. Countries that try to pursue liberal import policies without calling on foreign exporters to exercise voluntary restraint often find themselves flooded with imports because of the more restrictive policies of others. For instance, Canada, unprotected by restraint agreements, experienced a tremendous increase in textile imports in the first half of 1976, something like 52 per cent in volume terms. LDC textile exporters found it difficult to penetrate the EEC market further, as, in addition to the Multi-Fibre Agreement, the European market was protected by no fewer than thirteen textile bilateral restraint agreements. The Canadian authorities had no alternative but to invoke Article 19 of GATT, which meant that supplying countries were entitled to take retaliatory action. Another example relates to the problem of Japanese steel exports during 1977. As a result of strong pressure from the E.E.C., Japan agreed, under a 'voluntary' quota, to limit steel exports to the Community to four-fifths of their 1976 level. Whereupon U.S. steelmakers, alarmed at a possible diversion of Japanese steel to the U.S. market, applied to their government for retaliatory action. The cause for concern over these practices is that they take place outside of the framework of GATT's rules, they escape multilateral supervision and are liable to get out of hand and sow seeds of discord. Agreement is not going to be easy on this delicate issue; but it is fairly common ground that any internationally agreed safeguard device should conform to a standard of non-discrimination, be easy to invoke and be subject to more effective international surveillance. Negotiating postures on this issue are apt to be ambiguous because countries most in favour of effective safeguards today might, tomorrow, find themselves suitable targets of any agreed restrictive device as they in turn seek to increase their sales in other countries' markets.

As in previous rounds, tariffs will be the principal subject of negotiation. Some believe that tariff levels are now so low, at least in the industrialised countries, that little can be gained from further liberalisation in this area and that the focus should shift to NTBs. And, of course, it is well known that fluctuations in exchange rates far outweigh tariffs as a determinant of trade flows. However, for many commodities, old-fashioned tariffs still constitute substantial impediments to trade especially where strong competition exists between domestic and foreign producers. Tariffs do not need to be high to be restrictive. If cost functions for similar goods are nearly identical across countries, even low tariffs can prevent trade. Average levels of nominal duties (however weighted) can, of course, be misleading as to the room for negotiation, their protective effects and the consequences of their reduction. The amount of protection to domestic industry afforded by the tariff schedule of a country is better measured by the so-called effective tariff rates on value added. For example, suppose a domestic industry imports raw materials which are subject to a duty of 200 per cent and which constitute half of the value of the finished product. If the final product is subject to a tariff rate of 100 per cent that industry actually receives no protection at all: the duties on imported inputs equal in value the duties paid on the final product. On the other hand, if the duty on the raw materials were zero, the actual effective protection to the factors of production in the industry would be 200 per cent. The oddity of this situation is due to the fact that a

tariff on the final product of an industry is equivalent to a subsidy on domestic production, whereas tariffs on imported intermediate goods or inputs used in the processing industry are similar to indirect taxes as regards their impact on the costs of firms comprising the industry. The effective rate is an attempt to summarise in one figure the net protective effect of these opposing influences on the cost structure of a processing industry. A large volume of international trade consists, in fact, of intermediate goods that are used as inputs for the production of finished products. The rationale for the calculation of the effective rate is that (*a*) in a modern economy production typically takes place in a series of stages, each stage processing the output of the preceding one, (*b*) tariffs are levied at differential rates on inputs and final products. What is needed, therefore, is a measure of the protection to value added by domestic factors of production in each individual process.

Whereas, nominal tariff levels indicate the increased cost that the tariff structure imposes on the consumer in the protected market, effective rates highlight the production effects and costs of protection (i.e. the resource-allocation effects).

The effective rate of protection for an industry is an indication of the maximum proportion by which the domestic value of the factors used in an industry can exceed the value added in the absence of protection. The effective rate of protection provided to industry j, (E_j), is defined as

$$E_j = \frac{V_j - V_j^*}{V_j^*},$$

where V_j denotes domestic value added and V_j^* value added measured at free-trade world-market prices per unit of output. This is a general formulation of the concept of effective protection. Thus defined it can be used to measure the effect on domestic value added of all measures of national trade control such as import quotas, direct subsidies, exchange controls, etc., as well as tariffs. In practice, because of the difficulties in obtaining reliable data on non-tariff distortions, an alternative formulation is often used, specifically with respect to the protective effect of tariffs. This effective tariff rate can be written in input–output form as follows:

$$E_j = \frac{t_j - \sum_{i=1}^{n} a_{ij} t_i}{1 - \sum_{i=1}^{n} a_{ij}},$$

where E_j = the effective rate of tariff protection to industry j;
a_{ij} = the share of intermediate inputs, i, in the cost of industry j valued at world prices;
t_i = nominal tariff rate on input i, and
t_j = nominal tariff rate on output of industry j.
As the last formula indicates, an industry's effective tariff protection will be greater than that indicated by its nominal tariff protection whenever the nominal tariff rate on the industry's output exceeds the weighted average tariff on its

inputs. When the opposite situation prevails, i.e. imported inputs bear higher customs duties than the finished product, we have the phenomenon of 'negative value added'. Here the value of inputs exceeds the value of the finished product reckoned in world market prices. Negative value added is not a mere theoretical curiosity. The inefficiencies resulting from import-substitution policies in some countries, notably LDCs, have fostered productive activities that operate at negative value added. In such industries domestic resources are not only wasted, but their continued employment imposes real losses on the economy in terms of the opportunity costs of obtaining the same output. What is meant here is that it would be far cheaper for the country to import the finished product rather than attempt to make it at home. Domestic production at negative value added, although socially inefficient, can remain privately profitable only because costs and prices are grossly distorted by taxes and subsidies. In general the degree of protection an industry obtains from the tariff structure tends to be greater (1) the higher the nominal tariff rate on its output (2) the smaller the proportion of its value added per unit of output, and (3) the lower the nominal tariffs on the industry's inputs.[2]

The pattern of effective rates is useful information in the context of trade liberalisation, in that they show the extent to which different industries in a given country must reduce their production costs. The reduction of an industry's effective protection through cuts in nominal tariffs results in a decrease in its value added. Marginal firms might then go out of business if they are unable to cover their variable costs. The extent of the movement (and the associated adjustment problem) depends on the elasticity of supply of firms in the affected industry. The higher the elasticity of supply of firms in the industry, the greater the resource movement. Estimates of effective tariff protection in the E.E.C.[3] calculated with the aid of West German input—output figures indicate a great variability of effective rates. For manufacturing industry as a whole, the average nominal tariff is only 7.3 per cent and the average effective tariff is 10 per cent; but there are important industries where the effective rates are over 15 per cent and some 20 per cent (e.g. pulp and paper products, non-ferrous metals, textiles, clothing and leather goods). In addition, the E.E.C. tariff

structure exhibits escalation effects, common to most countries' tariff schedules: both nominal and effective rates escalate
with the stage of processing. Raw materials and intermediate
inputs (e.g. energy, iron, crude steel, non-ferrous metals, wood
and leather) are admitted duty free or have negligible tariffs but
duty rates on final manufactured products are quite steep. The
escalation effects are particularly marked in those industries
that suffer from severe import competition, e.g. raw-material
intensive and low-skill-intensive industries. To that extent the
tariff structure (assisted by non-tariff barriers) discriminates
against the unskilled-intensive, low-technology exports of
developing countries. However, in respect of the United States,
another study[4] based on an analysis of nominal tariffs for 180
manufacturing industries found no evidence that industries
experiencing severe import competition receive high nominal
tariff protection. It is commonly assumed that declining
industries, industries important to national security and those
able to exercise political influence are obvious candidates for
high tariff protection. But the evidence shows that the height of
an industry's tariff bears little or no relationship to these
characteristics. This surprising result for the United States is
not the isolated case of a seemingly indiscriminate tariff
structure. The structure of effective tariffs in the United
Kingdom works in exactly the same way.[5] Industries vulnerable to import competition, senile industries, those able to
muster the largest number of votes, etc., generally receive no
more tariff protection than efficient industries able to withstand international competition.

If foreign competition has little to do with the height of an
industry's tariff in the developed countries, what is the logic of
these countries' protective structures? The short answer is that
there is no logic: there is no consistent economic rationale for
existing protective structures. Some have argued that tariff
structures serve the purpose of income maintenance or employment protection for certain sectors of the economy. And,
indeed, the evidence indicates that low-wage industries (i.e.
unskilled labour-intensive) in developed countries tend to have
somewhat higher tariffs. The escalation of tariff structures
tends to encourage higher stages of fabrication and this
maintains the industrial base. But these are the manifest effects

of an existing tariff structure; they do not constitute rational-isations for the tariff pattern in the sense of policies consciously designed to bring about these effects. The truth is that in each country the existing tariff structure is a heritage from the past: the two World Wars and the Great Depression of the 1930s. In each country the tariff structure evolved in a haphazard manner, shaped by the vicissitudes of wartime dislocation, industrial fluctuations and unemployment. The dissipation of the protectionist pattern since the 1950s left the tariff contour pretty much the same, although at a very much lower level. The Kennedy Round, for instance, effected tariff reductions as great for industries with strong import competition as for other industries, albeit with some variations, i.e. the proportionate reductions tended to be smallest in low-skill-intensive in-dustries. These variations were particularly marked in the case of U.S. tariff cuts. The largest reductions were made in industries or product groups characterised by advanced tech-nology, high capital and/or skill intensity and the prevalence of multinational firms. The same pattern is apparent with respect to the inter-industry incidence of U.S. non-tariff barriers. A plausible explanation for this pattern of U.S. tariffs and recent changes in U.S. trade policy has been offered which takes account of the considerable influence of U.S. multinational corporations in the making of American trade policy.[6] These corporations are powerful forces behind liberal trade policies in the United States, at least in the industries where they predominate. Although organised labour in general, presses for protection, in instances where clashes of interests with the internationalist outlook of big business occur, the view of the latter usually prevail. In industries where multinational busi-ness interests are not directly involved (e.g. textiles, footwear and other low-technology activities) protectionist pressures remain unopposed. The result of these divergent influences is the curious blend of liberalism and protectionism which characterises present U.S. trade policy. No doubt the same pressure-group explanation applies to the commercial policies of other industrial countries. Trade policy is a decision process that is obviously influenced by pressure groups and changes in the international economic environment that expose some industries, firms and particular groups of workers to new trade and employment opportunities and challenges. Ever since the repeal of the English Corn Laws in the nineteenth century, trade policies in all countries have been determined in the same manner: the outcome of a clash of divergent interests responding to changing economic circumstances. Economists have generally neglected the study of the political sources of national trade policies;[7] this is patently untenable as a scientific approach in view of the growing politicisation of economic decision-making, including the evolution of international economic policy. In view of the above, it is not easy to predict the nature and extent of the reductions in protective structures which might result from the current trade talks. Particularly so, since tariff bargaining focusses on nominal tariffs. But several studies have shown that nominal tariff rates are generally highly correlated with effective rates even when non-tariff barriers are included in the effective rates.[8] Therefore, sufficiently deep cuts in nominal tariffs should result in substantial reductions in effective protection.

To allow tariff reduction to proceed, countries have to agree on a tariff-cutting formula: harmonisation *v*. linear reduction. The E.E.C. favours the first approach and the U.S. the latter. The relative merits of the two tariff cutting techniques were argued at length at the commencement of the Kennedy Round. In the end, the negotiating countries settled on the linear across-the-board formula having been persuaded that the traditional item-by-item method was too cumbersome, too time-consuming and was not likely to result in tariff reductions of sufficient depth and scope. However, the results produced by the across-the-board formula were not entirely satisfactory to all concerned. At the last minute, countries introduced 'exception lists' when they realised that there were marked imbalances in the concessions they made when evaluated on a country-by-country basis. The United States, for instance, felt compelled to withdraw fully or partially many of its tariff offers to Japan and the E.E.C. in last-minute adjustments. The same action was taken by some other countries. Undaunted by that experience, the United States is again proposing an across-the-board cut of up to 60 per cent in industrial tariffs. The E.E.C. rejects this approach in favour of a harmonisation procedure that would even out the peaks and troughs of a country's tariff structure through reduction of higher tariff rates by a larger proportion than that of lower rates – 'lopping off the peaks'. If, say, there was a range of tariffs of 10, 20 and 50 per cent, the Americans would say, 'let's cut all of them by half' and the range would become 5, 10 and 25 per cent. Under the harmonisation procedure, the 10 per cent rate would be cut by 10 per cent, the 20 per cent rate by 20 per cent, while the 50 per cent rate would be halved. The E.E.C. and other countries advocating the harmonisation of tariffs consider that the central problem in this field is the 'disparities' in the tariff structure of the major trading countries. In particular, the common external tariff (CET) of the E.E.C. which was originally developed through a process of averaging the tariffs of member countries has a more even rate structure than that of the United States. The U.S. tariff varies widely from item to item. With an average of 5.5 per cent, the U.S. tariff schedule ranges from zero to 50 per cent, while in the E.E.C. the average is 4.4 per cent with a range of zero to 14 per cent. Linear cuts would therefore reduce U.S. protection less than E.E.C. protection. Just as in the last Round, a compromise will be found between the two negotiating positions that would involve selective cuts aimed at a reduction of 50 per cent of each participant's *average* level of duties on all products, with strictly limited 'exceptions'. This compromise approach while toppling large U.S. tariffs which annoy the Europeans, would meet the U.S. aim of reducing the mid-range tariffs that predominate in Europe.

What about the developing countries' interests in the multilateral trade talks? These countries have pinned their hopes on the Generalised System of Preferences (GSP) under which most developed countries extend tariff preferences to LDC manufactured exports. But their interests are equally (perhaps better) served by participating fully in the GATT talks. Initially, the developing countries felt threatened by any significant tariff reductions among the developed countries, because MFN tariff cuts would automatically erode preference margins presently enjoyed by developing countries under the GSP. (The preference margin is the absolute difference between the MFN rate of duty and the preferential rate for the like product, and not the proportionate relation between those rates.) But it is now being realised that the potential gains from tariff cuts on a MFN basis would greatly exceed the loss on the GSP. The tangible benefits from the GSP are problematic because the individual schemes of countries granting preferences are by no means uniform as to coverage or impact. The GSP schemes, restricted or hedged about as they are by exclusions, quotas or 'ceilings', tend to defeat the purposes of such preferences. Moreover, whereas the GSP is only meant to be temporary, MFN tariff reductions are permanent, i.e. secured by 'binding' of the rates.

In the following sections the issues raised by the other thorny items on the agenda – non-tariff barriers and agriculture – are examined.

1.2 Non-Tariff Barriers

In the area of non-tariff barriers (NTBs) past trade negotiators have done little but shadow box. Whether they will be any more successful this time in coming to grips with the problem remains to be seen. There are several reasons why NTBs have eluded the net of international control:

(1) Trade negotiators have been too busy attacking tariff walls.

(2) The trade-restricting effects of NTBs are difficult to quantify.

(3) Many NTBs are only partially visible and where they are easily discernible, e.g. quotas on agricultural products, they enjoy a high degree of political immunity.

(4) Some NTBs are incorporated in national legislation to promote public health, safety and abate pollution. While not expressly designed to restrict trade (i.e. merely to reduce external consumption or production diseconomies) they sometimes have that incidental effect. Great variety in the minimum standards employed in different countries may compel a producer to comply with so many diverse regulations that it curtails his export opportunities.

(5) Some NTBs do not impede trade but instead unduly encourage it.

As tariff walls have tumbled, non-tariff barriers have become more evident. The removal of tariffs stimulated governments to introduce new forms of non-tariff protection or to extend old ones. Under existing GATT rules on NTBs it is more difficult to increase tariffs unilaterally than to raise NTBs because of exposure to the costs of retaliatory tariffs from other countries. The desire for greater levels of protection than those afforded by tariffs may have been stimulated by the system of fixed exchange rates which masked long-term structural changes in patterns of international specialisation and comparative advantage. The increased level of interdependence tends to magnify the trade effects of purely domestic policy. International trade has grown more rapidly than world output in recent years, resulting in increased 'openness' for national economies. Between 1960 and 1974 the volume of world production doubled. But in the same period the volume of world exports tripled. Although, of course, some countries display much more openness than others, openness – measured by the ratio of traded goods to total output – increased in every major industrial country since 1959. For instance, the index of openness for France increased from 0.13 in 1959 to 0.23 in 1974 and for the United Kingdom from 0.20 to 0.30 during the same period. As a consequence of these developments NTBs have been a source of growing complaint. As an indication GATT has compiled an inventory of 800 complaints on NTBs filed by member countries. GATT launched the first comprehensive examination into NTBs in 1967 and has identified some 27 different types of NTBs.

Because little information has been available on NTBs and because little was done about them in the previous negotiations it is useful to examine in some greater depth their nature and extent. The following covers the major ones (particularly as they apply to trade in industrial products).

QUOTAS OR QRs (QUANTITATIVE RESTRICTIONS)

These are the most trade-distorting practices in use, e.g. widespread in trade in such products as foodstuffs, coal, cotton textiles, steel. The extent of industrial quotas is suggested by Table 1.2 based on 1970 data. A quota system operates by

Table 1.2

Industrial Import Quotas in Major Countries, 1970

	Value of industrial imports subject to QRs	Percentage of industrial imports subject to QRs
E.E.C.	$ 900m.	4.3
United Kingdom	$ 700m.	4.7
Japan	$1400m.	11.4
United States	$5100m.	16.5

Source: *U.S. International Economic Policy in an Interdependent World* (Washington, D.C.: U.S. Government Printing Office, 1971) p. 667.

prohibiting, often from specified sources, the import of a good beyond a certain amount during a particular time period. Instead of, or in addition to, quotas a type of QR becoming rather fashionable is the voluntary restraint agreement whereby foreign exporters, usually under the threat of some action, agree to limit their exports to the domestic market. While tariffs reduce the benefits of comparative advantage, QRs nullify it, except within the permitted value of imports. When the quota maximum is reached, and no more imports are allowed in, the price connection between countries breaks. Within the maximum limit it is always possible to determine a tariff equivalent, i.e. a tariff rate that would produce the same result for domestic producers. The difference between domestic and world market prices (calculated as a percentage of world market prices) is the tariff equivalent. The welfare cost of quotas can be quite considerable. For the United States the cost of import quotas and voluntary restraints on six items account for most of the total cost of U.S. protection.[9]

SUBSIDIES

Government subsidies, either for domestic sales or for export, clearly affect international competition. When a subsidy is paid to domestic producers (at the expense of domestic consumers and taxpayers) it may block imports as effectively as a tariff. A direct subsidy on exports is, of course, the opposite of a tax on imports and thus provides the exporter with a competitive advantage. This competitive edge can enable such an exporter to win a certain share of the international market formerly served by foreign firms. GATT rules out direct export subsidies (except on primary products) and at least among some developed countries general export subsidies are resorted to only temporarily for balance of payments reasons. But more serious than direct subsidies on export sales are the wide variety of permanent export subsidising techniques currently in use. The field of export credit subsidies, for example, has shown marked growth. The United States provides credit at below-market rates of interest to exporters of American products through the operation of the Export—Import Bank. The same is done in Belgium, France and the United Kingdom. In Britain loans from the Export Credit Guarantee Department (ECGD) have long been available for foreign buyers of British ships at favourable rates of interest. The Common Market Countries have recently (April 1977) moved to restore some kind of order in this field and to prevent growing cut-throat competition among themselves in the granting of export credits. The move is aimed at making obligatory on members the observance of the voluntary OECD guidelines on export credits. The imposition of mandatory controls (in the form of permissible minimum interest rates and repayment periods) followed complaints that Italy had broken the voluntary guidelines by granting very generous export credits on the sale of tankers to the Soviet Union. Other techniques include the granting of special tax advantages to firms that increase their exports significantly. The way different national tax structures affect trade is illustrated by the important controversy that has developed over the impact of the E.E.C.'s border taxes. Border taxes are indirect taxes (e.g. VAT in Europe) and under GATT rules such taxes can be rebated to exporters, unlike direct taxes which cannot. American businessmen, who are mainly subject to direct taxes, claim such a system gives European exporters an unfair competitive advantage. The Americans, in turn, have been attacked in the trade talks for giving a tax subsidy to their own exporters through the Domestic International Sales Corporations (DISCs). The device is a disguised border tax adjustment. The creation of DISCs was provided for under the

Revenue Act of 1971. The intention was to put U.S. export sales on a more nearly equal footing with U.S. foreign corporations in terms of tax treatment, thereby slowing the trend towards the establishment of foreign subsidiaries by American corporations and increasing direct exports from the United States. U.S. firms can organise their export operations under a DISC subsidiary and gain 50 per cent remission of taxes on profits from export sales. But the United States is not the only offender. Most industrial countries tax profits earned on the export of manufactured goods at lower effective rates than they tax profits earned on domestic sales. In Ireland, for instance, export profits are simply not taxed. The treatment of export profits in many countries is part of a broader tendency to replace tariff barriers with fiscal protection.[10]

GOVERNMENT PROCUREMENT POLICIES

Most governments when purchasing supplies give some sort of preference to domestic suppliers over foreign suppliers. In the United States, under the Buy American Act of 1933, domestic producers get government contracts if their prices are within 6–12 per cent of the highest foreign bids. In addition, the Defence Department applies a 50 per cent differential. The United States for its part complains that other countries — unlike the United States — do not spell out the rules so that American firms know what they are up against when trying to compete with local suppliers. Little action is likely on government procurement policies in the current trade talks since this item has been dropped from the agenda.

ADMINISTRATIVE AND TECHNICAL REGULATIONS

There are many variations on this theme. These include health, safety and anti-pollution standards (e.g. safety regulations for machines and pollution control for cars), customs valuation practices, anti-dumping laws and procedures for applying countervailing duties. A countervailing duty is an import charge designed to offset an export subsidy by another country, including rebates on exports connected with indirect taxes (VAT in particular) and all the forms of relief that reduce industrial costs, especially in depressed areas. An American practice under this heading that particularly annoys other countries is the customs valuation procedure known as the American Selling Price (ASP) which applies to four groups of products (benzenoid chemicals, rubber-soled footwear, canned clams and certain wool-knit gloves). Under ASP U.S. imports are valued for tariff purposes at the selling price of similar products produced in the United States rather than at the export value of the foreign-made product. Since the former price is usually higher than the export price the duties paid may be considerably higher than the former tariff schedule. In effect ASP acts as a variable levy on the relevant exports to the United States. No other major trading country uses an import valuation system based on domestic prices. American tariff schedules differ, too, from the Brussels Tariff Nomenclature (BTN) which is used by more than 100 countries. The special classification used by the United States, apart from allowing an arbitrary valuation of imports such as ASP, is also unnecessarily complex in that it provides for some nine different methods of establishing the value of articles. Procedures for applying anti-dumping and countervailing duties (to counteract price discrimination and subsidy programmes of other governments, respectively) differ among countries, and in some cases are unnecessarily protracted. The delays and uncertainties involved set obstacles in the way of international commerce. U.S. countervailing duty practice provides for no 'injury' requirement as called for under GATT rules.

It is obvious from this brief survey of some typical NTBs that their elimination is going to be a more complex undertaking than tariff reduction. What is required among the trading nations is no small effort. It is no less than the generation of a collective will to renounce the apparatus of the new mercantilism. There are no signs or indications that governments are ready to make this commitment, even on a multilateral basis. Throughout the industrial world government intervention in the market-place in pursuit of separate national goals such as full employment, regional development, industrial organisation and environmental control has spawned the multifarious NTBs that are so firmly entrenched that a general retreat would be regarded by the national beneficiaries of industrial public assistance as an abdication of national economic sovereignty. However, the pressure of events in the field of international competition is forcing governments to face up to the mutually damaging consequences of national NTBs. Individual governments seem more inclined to negotiate over sensitive issues for fear of provoking countermeasures from other countries. For instance, the E.E.C. and Japan have been engaged in delicate talks to avert a threatened trade war over the use of NTBs in shipbuilding and steel – industries plagued by intense competition and weak demand. Should this conciliatory attitude carry over to the Geneva trade talks, some progress might be achieved if only in the form of a code of behaviour on NTBs.

1.3   Agricultural Protectionism

It was recalled earlier in this chapter that the Kennedy Round almost foundered on the inability of the E.E.C. and the United States to settle on trade in temperate-zone agricultural products (food and feed grains, sugar, dairy products and meat). Now that negotiating positions on this delicate issue are better known it is unlikely that a similar clash would develop detrimental to progress in the industrial sector. But by the same token it is wishful thinking to expect any significant agreement to emerge from the Tokyo Round tending to reduce agricultural trade barriers. World agriculture is in an endemic state of disarray and will remain so for many more years to come. Like NTBs, the level of agricultural protectionism has increased, responding to political and social pressures from domestic producers (i.e. farm lobbies) and other advocates of national interest. Yet the gains to the world economy, and to individual countries, from a more rational pattern of specialisation and trade in agricultural products can be enormous, perhaps surpassing the benefits from the elimination of all NTBs. According to one source the cost of agricultural protectionism in the form of income and price-support measures to farmers in the principal developed countries amounted to at least $30,000m. annually in 1973. A rough idea of the extent of agricultural protectionism is suggested by Table 1.3 based on 1970 data.

Table 1.3

Agricultural Import Quotas in Major Countries, 1970

Country	Value of agricultural imports subject to QRs and variable levies	Percentage of total agricultural imports covered by quotas and variable levies
United States	$1200m.	21.6
United Kingdom	$1100m.	21.9
Japan	$ 800m.	27.9
E.E.C.	$2600m.	33.7

Source: *U.S. International Economic Policy*, p. 671.

The American negotiators are leading the fight for a more liberal trade pattern in temperate-zone agriculture. The United States with its undoubted comparative advantage in farm products (e.g. the United States is the leading wheat-exporting country accounting for 35 per cent of the wheat entering world trade) is assigning high priority to agriculture in the trade talks with particular focus on the Common Agricultural Policy (CAP) variable levy system of the EEC.[11] That system is designed to ensure the internal sale of major E.E.C. agricultural products. As international commodity prices drop the variable levy rises in order to prevent foreign producers from increasing their sales. As this system maintains internal prices well above world levels provision is made for export subsidies when surpluses develop. The disposal of these surpluses abroad, often backed by high subsidies, disrupts the traditional markets of efficient producers such as the United States, Canada and Australia. For instance, in 1973 the E.E.C. exported subsidised butter to the Soviet Union at a price of 1.9 French francs per kilogram – compared with the world price of 3 francs per kilogram and a price of 10.33 francs per kilogram paid to butter producers in the Community. An enormous dairy surplus in 1976 produced another butter mountain in Europe; and there were reports early in 1977 that 10,000 tonnes of subsidised butter were sold to the Soviet Union. The proliferation of variable levies and export subsidies – not only in the E.E.C. – has undoubtedly increased instability on the world market. Under these conditions equilibrium prices that can clear markets do not exist: large sectors of the world market are officially controlled. The overall result has been seriously to curb the operation of market forces, thereby restricting and distorting agricultural trade.

U.S. officials are putting the emphasis in the current negotiations on the necessity of opening up markets for efficient producers. They argue that the benefits of trade liberalisation exist as much in agriculture as in industry. They point out that agriculture is as much an industry as any manufacturing activity in the sense that it transforms inputs into finished products often with the aid of sophisticated techniques of production. The adjustment problems in agriculture are the same as in industry. Consequently the Americans argue that the agreed tariff-cutting formula should be applied as generally as possible and should include, in particular, tariff cuts on agricultural products. In this view substantial liberalisation in agricultural trade would be more likely if industrial and agricultural tariff reductions were combined in a single package. Similarly, the negotiations on NTBs should encompass non-tariff barriers both in agriculture and industry. By contrast, the E.E.C. position is to treat agricultural questions separately. According to the E.E.C., both tariff and non-tariff restrictions on agricultural trade should be considered in the group on agriculture. The Tokyo Declaration which launched the current Round indeed mentions 'the special characteristics of problems in this (i.e. agricultural) sector'. Recent developments in production and trade illustrate that the agricultural sector is by nature subject to variations — especially in production (or on the supply side) — which in turn lead to variations on world markets and therefore in trade. For instance, the sharp increases in world food prices during 1972–4, largely explained by poor harvests in the Soviet Union and in Southern Asia, have recently given way to declining prices as a result both of record U.S. harvests and big crops elsewhere. Farming interests in the United States are now advocating higher support prices and tighter production controls. If past experience is any guide this can only lead to mountains of unsold farm commodities on world markets.

These abrupt changes in market conditions illustrate in the E.E.C.'s view the 'specificity' of the agricultural sector. The E.E.C. countries therefore consider that the approach to the negotiations should aim primarily to create – while respecting existing policies – the conditions for a better-adapted supply which would make possible an evolution of world markets more satisfactory both to importers and exporters. To give practical expression to this the E.E.C. urges the implementation of the 1974 World Food Conference call for an international system of nationally held grain reserves for the dual purposes of famine relief and of stabilising world markets. The United States appears ready to respond and to join with the other major exporting countries and the importing countries to hold stocks of grain with an equitable sharing of costs in order to achieve a significant degree of trade liberalisation.

The European preference is for a managed system with international commodity arrangements for grain and dairy products; this clashes with American insistence on free trade in agriculture. The CAP may be protectionist, yet the E.E.C. remains the world's largest importer of food and feedstuffs. In 1975 the Community had an overall farm trade deficit of more than $21.5 billion, with U.S. exports of farm products accounting for $5.6 billion of the total, providing the United States with a $4.5 billion surplus on farm trade with the Nine. Over the past six years American agricultural exports to the E.E.C. have risen by 170 per cent in value terms. The E.E.C. is, therefore, critical of the general negotiating stance of the United States.[12] E.E.C. officials point out that U.S. enthusiasm for a liberal trading regime in agriculture is highly selective, applying mainly to those products in which the United States has a comparative advantage, while in regard to agricultural commodities in which it is uncompetitive, or needs imports, its policies are at least as protective as those of the E.E.C. The European feeling is that the United States is purposely treating agricultural trade as a one-way flow. While the Community has stuck to its GATT commitment to allow U.S. soya beans and soya bean meal duty-free access, E.E.C. dairy products (beef and canned hams) have been pushed out of the American market by a rigid system of quotas. European agricultural products also face considerable barriers in other important markets; for instance, Japan maintains quota restrictions on more than twenty agricultural items.

The way forward is for the E.E.C., the United States and other key participants to put up all or substantially all of their agricultural border protection for concessionary bargaining. If the United States offers a progressive liberalisation or elimination of its quantitative restrictions on certain dairy products, cotton, wheat, sugar, etc., and agrees to limit its own agricultural export subsidy programmes, then the E.E.C. might be induced to concede a modification of the CAP's variable levy system. For instance, limits might be set on the levels of the variable levies; and, over a number of years, there could be a phased replacement of the threshold prices which trigger the levies with agreed fixed tariffs. Progress along these lines would naturally disturb or undermine basic domestic farm policies and this would be an advantage because ultimately what is required is a change in farm policies themselves. For the E.E.C. this would imply a change in CAP. Critics of the CAP would like to see a shift away from the price support policy (through a gradual lowering of prices) towards direct income payments to the Community's farmers. The E.E.C. might be heading in this direction anyway despite a negotiating position that takes existing farm policies for granted and not as the subject for international negotiation. Consumer dissatisfaction with high food prices within the Community, huge surpluses of certain foodstuffs and the meagre results of the CAP in achieving its stated objectives have combined to set in motion a fundamental reappraisal of the CAP within the E.E.C. Commission. In 1976 the E.E.C.'s prices for wheat were 124 per cent higher than world prices, 158 per cent higher for beef and veal and 320 per cent higher for butter. Poor farmers have not benefited either. The evidence suggests that the gap between rich and poor farmers continues to grow and the drift from the land has not been arrested. Ultimately the CAP will have to change for it is becoming increasingly clear that it is a 'Kulak's Chapter', i.e. it benefits the most prosperous farmers – not consumers or small farmers.

Multilateral discussions on agricultural protectionism are certain to continue for many more years to come. The issues involved would continue to challenge the skills of commercial diplomacy. Only if substantial changes occur in domestic farm policies would the benefits of comparative advantage and efficient resource allocation in agriculture spread to consumers throughout the world.

Further Reading

R. E. Baldwin, *Non-tariff Distortions of International Trade* (Washington, D. C.: The Brookings Institution, 1970). The standard treatment of NTBs. Particularly good on quotas.

C. F. Bergsten (ed.), *The Future of the International Economic Order: An Agenda for Research* (Farnborough: D. C. Heath, 1974).

H. Corbet and R. Jackson (eds), *In Search of a New World Economic Order* (New York: Halsted Press, Wiley, 1974). Fifteen papers on the issues and problems arising in the Multilateral Trade Negotiations.

D. G. Johnson, *World Agriculture in Disarray* (London: Macmillan, 1973).

W. F. Monroe, *International Trade Policy in Transition* (Lexington, Mass.: Lexington Books, 1975).

B. Södersten, *International Economics* (London: Macmillan, 1971) part iv, chaps 19–22.

CHAPTER 2

Trade and Debt Problems of the Third World

2.1 Expansion of Industrial Exports

LDCs are becoming increasingly conscious of the limitations of an industrialisation strategy based on import substitution (building up local industry behind tariff walls). For many of the smaller LDCs import substitution results in a gross misallocation of resources, discrimination against exports and widespread production at negative value added. As a consequence there has been a marked shift in focus. They have adopted a variety of measures to promote industrial exports. The reason for this shift in emphasis is that the package of policies used to stimulate import substitution discriminates significantly against the development of export production. This discrimination exists for a variety of reasons. The import regime (based on tariffs, quotas and exchange controls) typically allows a country to balance its international payments at a higher exchange rate than would be possible with a more liberal policy. Thus, regardless of whether the trade and exchange barriers were erected primarily to protect domestic industry as part of an import substitution strategy or merely to conserve foreign exchange or to provide government revenue, the effect in all cases is to overvalue the exchange rate. An overvalued exchange rate discourages manufactured exports in at least three ways:

(1) It reduces the profitability of exporting as an activity. The domestic currency value of foreign exchange earnings are reduced below the rate that would be set by a more appropriate exchange rate. Imported inputs or domestically produced import-competing inputs have to be purchased by the export

industries at above world prices. In many countries this contributes to an 'inefficiency illusion', i.e. because domestic production costs exceed world prices, the impression is created that local industry cannot compete or export without protection.

(2) It provides an environment for a protected industry to tolerate relatively more inefficiency than an unprotected one. Slack management, underutilised capacity, unexploited economies of scale often prevent firms from exporting their output.

(3) Existing export opportunities may not be grasped because production for the protected domestic market is typically more profitable and assured.

In addition, other features of an import-substitution strategy militate against exports. Import-substitution policies typically include low or zero tariffs on imports of capital equipment. Combined with relatively high industrial wages, this encourages the establishment of capital-intensive industries and the use of capital-intensive techniques which are often quite inappropriate for the development of export markets. In this connection Thomas K. Morrison's demonstration[1] that high levels of protection discourage manufactured exports in LDCs deserves attention. In a cross-country analysis of the export performance of eighteen to forty-five LDCs he found that nominal tariff levels were negatively and, the 'openness' of an economy, positively related to manufacturing export performance. For his sample of forty-five countries his results indicated that a 10 per cent increase in the 'openness' of an economy (measured by an incremental import/consumption ratio) was associated with a 15 per cent increase in manufactured exports as a proportion of manufacturing output.

These problems relating to the industrial export sector can be solved by devaluing the exchange rate to a more appropriate level while removing quantitative import controls and reducing tariffs. Ideally, the reduction of trade barriers could be accomplished within the current Tokyo Round and depreciation effected forthwith. However, while some LDCs have experimented with floating or frequent devaluations and have indicated a desire to liberalise trade in multilateral negotiations, the majority of LDCs are still too firmly wedded to protection as a way of life for one to expect much movement in this direction. Once an industrial structure geared to import substitution has been established changes become increasingly difficult. In practice exchange rate policy is subject to a particularly rigid set of constraints in LDCs whose exports still consist essentially of primary products (up to 85 per cent). With low price elasticity of demand for these products there is a terms of trade argument for keeping an overvalued exchange rate to maximise export receipts. For instance, in Colombia exchange rate policy throughout the post-war period has been governed very strongly by the need to maximise export receipts from the sale of coffee. The exchange rate that the Colombian authorities deemed appropriate for the coffee sector has not always been adequate for the promotion of industrial exports.

As an alternative to more liberal trade and exchange policies developing countries can counteract the negative effects of protection by means of various export-promotion schemes. These are basically subsidies to exporters designed to offset the 'tax' which overvalued exchange rates and protection places on LDC exporters. Examples of export incentives are: (*a*) export grants and exemption from export taxes (designed to increase the gross receipts from exports), (*b*) subsidies on labour use and other inputs, credit subsidies (designed to reduce the exporter's costs), (*c*) tax advantages, (*d*) remission of import duties and exemption from exchange controls. These export promotion measures sometimes combined with periodic currency devaluations have enabled some countries, e.g. Mexico, Brazil, Taiwan and South Korea, to obtain a rapid and sustained growth of exports.

But there is the danger of overkill in an export-oriented strategy, i.e. LDCs can err on the side of too much chaotic intervention to boost exports. Since import-substitution activities (supported by the panoply of QRs, exchange controls, high tariffs, etc.) exist even in the outward-looking LDCs there is no guarantee that every movement towards export promotion results in a more efficient allocation of resources. Ideally the marginal cost of earning foreign exchange (through export promotion) should be equated to the marginal cost of saving foreign exchange (through import substitution). However, because (a) export incentives are so varied, (b) they have evolved in a haphazard and piecemeal fashion over the years, and (c) there is a need to favour indirect rather than outright export subsidies so as to get around GATT rules (Article 16) on export subsidisation and avoid retaliation by importing countries, they are often difficult to analyse and compare on a cost-benefit basis. Yet some assessment of the various export-subsidising techniques is required for rational policy making, e.g. how the production incentives affect production for the export market versus the domestic market, how the relative incentives vary among industries, etc. On the basis of such information an incentive structure can be developed that promotes a more efficient use of scarce resources. At least to start with, estimates should be made of the effective rates of export subsidy (analogous to the effective tariff protection concept). The effective rate of export subsidy is defined as the percentage excess of value added measured in domestic prices (V_d) over value added in world prices (V_w), which is equivalent to the net subsidy (S) as a percentage of value added in world prices, i.e.

the effective rate of subsidy (ERS)

$$= \frac{V_d - V_w}{V_w} . 100$$

$$= \frac{[(V_w + S) - V_w]}{V_w} . 100 = \frac{S}{V_w} . 100$$

Estimates of effective rates of subsidy to different industries can then be used to (a) detect cases of excessive subsidisation, (b) equalise the incentive provided to the export sector with tariff protection afforded to import replacement activities. Studies undertaken by the U.S. National Bureau of Economic Research (NBER) on exchange control, liberalisation and economic development[2] over the last few years, and the ongoing research on export-promotion policies of a number of developing countries by the World Bank indicate potential benefits from an export-oriented development strategy. Export-promotion strategies generally appear to have higher pay-offs than those of one-sided import-substitution policies.

Gearing up for an expansion of industrial exports is one problem for LDCs; another problem is adequate access to markets. Spokesmen for developing countries loudly complain that despite determined efforts to alter the structure of their economies along comparative advantage lines, they still do not obtain adequate access to developed countries' markets for their labour-intensive low-technology exports. Table 2.1 shows

Table 2.1

Imports of Manufactures* by 21 Developed Countries from Developing Countries, 1962, 1973

	1962	1973
Imports from LDCs ($ million)	2482.3	15,920.0
LDC percentage share in total imports	5.0	6.3

* Includes food products, drink and tobacco products, wood products and furniture, rubber products, leather and footwear, textiles, clothing, chemicals, pulp, paper and board, nonmetallic mineral products, iron and steel, worked nonferrous metals, road motor vehicles, other engineering and metal products, and miscellaneous light manufactures. Excludes petroleum products and unworked nonferrous metals.

Source: UNCTAD, *Trade in Manufactures of Developing Countries and Territories, 1974 Review*, document TD/B/C. 2/161, United Nations Publications, table 7, p. 13.

that the LDC percentage share in total imports of selected groups of manufactures into developed countries amounts to a paltry 6.3 per cent – an increase of only 1.6 per cent over the LDC share more than a decade ago. While a handful of LDCs (Hong Kong, Singapore, Brazil, Mexico, Korea, etc.) have been remarkably successful in penetrating industrial markets – see Table 2.2 – this very success tends to generate restrictive reactions in the trade policies of the developed countries additional to those already in force. Additionally the escalated structure of protection (as against its level) in the developed countries discourages the expansion of processing industries in LDCs. The escalated pattern of the industrial countries' tariffs is apparent from the tariff profiles in Table 2.3 (the tendency for higher tariffs to apply as the stage of processing advances).

Table 2.2

Leading Developing Country Exporters of Manufactures, 1970, 1972

Country	Value of manufactured exports ($ million)	
	1970	1972
Hong Kong	1949	3233
Republic of Korea	641	1359
Israel	540	847
Pakistan	397	376
India	1081	1028
Mexico	391	647
Singapore	428	890
Egypt	205	256
Argentina	246	381
Brazil	363	736
Total	6241	9753
Total LDCs	8905	15,623
Percentage of ten LDCs in total LDC exports of manufactures	71	62.4

Source: UNCTAD, *The Second United Nations Development Decade. Trends and Policies in the First Two Years.* Background papers presented by the Secretary-General of UNCTAD for the first review and appraisal of the implementation of the International Development Strategy, part 2, table 14, p. 84; and UNCTAD, *Review of International Trade and Development, 1975*, document TD/B/530/Add. 1/Rev. 1, part 1, table xviii, p. 35.

Thus, in most developed countries, while hides and skins are admitted duty free, tariffs on leather products are high, e.g. in the United States, 16.4 per cent on finished leather goods and 10.6 per cent on leather footwear. The same cascaded effect, to a lesser or greater degree, is apparent on the processing of a wide range of industrial supplies and raw materials. This means, as we have seen, that effective rates of tariff protection on finished products substantially exceed the nominal rates. In the E.E.C., for instance, effective rates exceed nominal rates by 30 per cent on average. The discriminatory effect can be extremely powerful on the imports of labour-intensive, low-technology products in which LDCs have comparative advan-

Table 2.3

Industrial Tariff Profiles in Selected Major Industrial Countries

	Industrial supplies	Semi-finished goods	Manufactured products
	%	%	%
United States	2.5	5.6	8.8
Japan	3.4	6.3	12.7
E.E.C.	0.4	4.8	8.2

Source: *Tariff Information*, Ministry of International Trade and Industry, Japan, 1974.

Tariff rates are weighted averages of those on individual commodities within each commodity group in effect as of 1 January 1972.

tage (textiles, footwear, rugs, handbags, processed foodstuffs, etc.).

To overcome these restrictive tariff barriers, LDCs (under the inspired leadership of Raúl Prebisch, the first Secretary-General of UNCTAD) pressed in 1964 for a general system of preferential (GSP) tariff rates by developed countries favouring their manufactured and semi-manufactured imports. Wrapped up as a variant of the classical 'infant-industry argument', the GSP was sold to the developed countries as constituting an important incentive for LDCs to overcome their inward looking import-substitution policies and to increase their foreign exchange earnings through a sufficiently large and sustained expansion of manufactured exports. The first ten year preferential tariff scheme came into operation in 1971[3] and by 1976 all the developed countries that had agreed to provide preferential treatment had done so: E.E.C., Japan, Norway (1971); Denmark, Finland, New Zealand, Sweden, Switzerland, Austria (1972); Canada (1974); United States (1976).

However, performance failed to live up to promise or expectation. The schemes actually in operation are emasculated versions of the original proposals and seem hardly to justify the time and effort expended in their creation. As previously noted, the various schemes suffer from severe limitations imposed by the donor countries to blunt the effects on domestic industry of unrestricted imports from developing countries. These can be conveniently noted under the headings of product coverage, margins of preference and safeguard mechanisms.

PRODUCT COVERAGE

All the schemes cover manufactures and semi-manufactures, a limited number of primary commodities and a few agricultural and fishery products. However, textiles, leather and leather products are excluded; in effect, preferential treatment is withheld from 62 per cent of all dutiable manufactured imports from LDCs. Clearly, the exclusion of such a large volume of manufactured imports from the GSP has limited its credibility as an effective programme for promoting manufactured exports of LDCs. In fact, it has been observed that the preference scheme of one of the most important donors (the E.E.C.) 'is designed for goods in which the developing countries cannot, or not yet, compete'.[4] In 1976 (the first year of operation of the American preferential scheme) 11 per cent of total U.S. imports from eligible countries entered duty free under the GSP. The developing countries exported $28,498m. to the United States, of which $3,160m. managed to satisfy the GSP requirements. Products covered by the GSP comprise only 2 per cent of the total imports of the donor countries.

PREFERENCE MARGINS

Duty-free treatment is accorded to manufactures covered by the schemes of the E.E.C., the Nordic countries and the United States. With the exception of some textile products, clothing and footwear, on which a 50 per cent reduction of MFN rate applies, Japan admits LDC manufactures duty-free. Canada grants a 33 per cent preference margin. Austria and Switzerland apply a 30 per cent reduction.

SAFEGUARD MECHANISMS

Fear of structural unemployment in the developed world as a

result of imports from low-wage countries, unallayed by any coherent policy programmes of adjustment assistance by the governments concerned, has resulted in very stringent safeguard measures being attached to the GSP. Most donor countries safeguard their threatened markets through a standard escape clause modelled on GATT's Article 19 whereby donor countries can withhold preferential treatment totally or partially when imports threaten or cause serious injury to domestic producers. The E.E.C. and Japan, by contrast, protect 'exposed' domestic industries by placing ceilings on preferential imports – in effect through tariff quotas. Under these systems imports in excess of the ceilings are charged MFN rather than GSP rates. In the case of the E.E.C. the volume of duty-free trade (i.e. the ceilings) was determined by the volume of the Community's imports from the favoured LDCs in 1968[5] plus 5 per cent of the volume of its imports from all other countries. Each beneficiary LDC cannot supply more than 50 per cent of each product's duty-free quota. For 'sensitive' products the country's share is even smaller for some items, i.e. 20–30 per cent of the total. Obviously, if there are only one or two major suppliers, and other beneficiary countries cannot take up the part of the quota reserved for them, then part of the ceiling is sterilised, thereby reducing the total benefit of the GSP. The suspicion is therefore aroused that the purpose of this regulation is to limit the imports of those products for protectionist reasons rather than to give the least-developed LDCs a better chance to penetrate the E.E.C. market. However one cares to regard it, the application of this formula is so restrictive that little expansion of preferential trade is likely.

In addition to these basic features which restrict the trade creation effect of the GSP, the schemes are further circumscribed by strict rules of origin and the exclusion of some important suppliers from the list of beneficiary countries. The rules of origin exclude from preferential treatment clothing manufactured from imported textiles or radios assembled using imported transistors. Under the U.S. scheme proof is required that at least 35 per cent of the import value of any eligible product was added in the country claiming GSP treatment. The requirement that goods must be consigned directly from the exporting to the importing country makes it more difficult for landlocked countries to take advantage of the scheme. The preferences are, in general, extended to members of the so-called Group of 77 (in fact, over 100 LDCs). However, each donor reserves the right to exclude any country from its list of beneficiaries. Thus, the U.S. scheme excludes Communist countries (unless they are members of international organisations like IMF or GATT) and members of OPEC. Mediterranean countries enjoying preferential status *vis-à-vis* the E.E.C. are also excluded from the U.S. list. Preferential treatment in the U.S. scheme does not apply to imports of a commodity from a particular LDC if that country supplies 50 per cent of the total value of U.S. imports of $25m. annually of the commodity. In many other schemes certain important LDC suppliers of textiles are excluded.

Estimates[6] have been made of the static trade-flow effects of the GSP using the standard tools of customs union theory — trade creation and trade diversion. The net trade creation effect is the difference between the increase in beneficiary countries' exports (trade creation or newly created trade) and the decline in developed countries' exports (trade diversion or displaced exports) resulting from the preferences. Net trade creation can be taken as a measure of the beneficial (welfare) effects of the GSP and an indication of improved global allocative efficiency. The results are presented in Table 2.4 based on 1971 trade data and estimated export supply and import demand elasticities. The beneficial effects are meagre indeed.

Without quota restrictions and exclusions the calculations indicate that developed countries' exports of the items covered by preferences fall by $380m., while LDC exports rise by $1386m. resulting in a global trade creation of $1006m, or just over 4 per cent of the developed countries' imports of eligible products. The addition of quantitative restrictions (tariff quotas) and exclusions which normally prevail reduces the estimated net trade creation to $233m. or less than 1 per cent of developed countries' imports of eligible commodities in 1971. Such insignificant trade expansion effects can do little to generate incentives for encouraging manufactured exports from LDCs. Indeed, some analysts regard the GSP as a

Table 2.4

Trade Creation Effects of Tariff Cuts and Quantitative Limitations Under the GSP Schemes (1971 data, in thousand U.S. dollars)

Donor Countries	Tariff cuts only		Tariff cuts and quantitative limitations	
	Trade creation	Trade creation as percentage of donor country's imports	Trade creation	Trade creation as percentage of donor country's imports
Australia	5788	0.78	2840	0.38
Austria	1934	0.27	577	0.08
Canada	16,477	0.85	2975	0.15
E.E.C.	111,805	3.04	20,731	0.29
Japan	51,859	5.29	1651	0.17
New Zealand	5610	2.83	5439	2.75
Nordic countries	21,463	0.97	11,272	0.51
Switzerland	4725	0.36	4346	0.33
United States	678,632	7.94	183,037	2.14
Total	1,006,368	4.22	232,868	0.98

Source: Adapted from table 2, p. 38, Z. Iqbal, 'The Generalised System of Preferences Examined', *Finance and Development*, vol. 12, no. 3 (Sept 1975).

programme of 'aid' rather than 'trade'.[7] Even so, the aid (in the form of revenue transfers, reckoned as the tariff revenue forgone by the donors on the ceiling level of imports) based on the estimated results reported above, amounts to less than 5 per cent of the external assistance provided by the developed countries. To change the GSP from an aid to a trade programme some basic alterations are required, viz:

(1) The removal or liberalisation of the built-in quantitative restrictions (tariff quotas, etc.) so as to create price incentives at the margin for LDC exports.

(2) The addition to the lists of eligible items to include goods such as textiles, leather, agricultural products and other products in which LDCs specialise.

(3) The binding of the preferential margins or tariffs under GATT.

Although the Third World is pressing for far-reaching modifications in the existing preference schemes it is doubtful, in the present climate of protectionism, whether this demand would be met with any sympathetic response from the developed world. The developing countries are, in fact, barking up the wrong tree. The failure of the preference scheme is the failure of the rich countries to cope with the problems of adjustment to changing patterns of comparative advantage. The restrictive quotas, ceilings, voluntary restraint agreements and the high effective protection on labour-intensive products are merely defensive mechanisms to avoid the severe social and economic costs of structural adjustment in the threatened areas and sectors of the developed countries. Rather than relying on preferences Third World countries would do better to concentrate their efforts through active participation in the GATT multilateral trade negotiations on (*a*) attacking QRs (NTBs in general), (*b*) pressing for deeper-than-average tariff cuts on a MFN basis (i.e. to all LDCs including those not eligible for preferences) and (*c*) establishing guidelines on effective adjustment assistance policies in developed countries. Recent estimates[8] indicate that the gains from a 50 per cent MFN tariff reduction could amount to four times the loss of GSP advantages due to the erosion of preferential margins ($32m. loss in annual trade flow from erosion of preferential margins, compared with $133m. trade expansion from multilateral tariff reductions).

Tinkering with the system through revisions to the GSP will not improve the chances of market access. In a sense the GSP only redresses the balance in favour of the LDCs resulting from the skewed distribution of Kennedy Round tariff cuts. As long as high effective tariff rates on products of export interest to the LDCs remain in force, QRs and voluntary restraints are not lifted and developed countries do not implement effective adjustment programmes, so long will market access for LDCs remain a problem. On the average, 20.9 per cent of LDC goods imported into the industrial countries are subject to NTBs, ranging from 3.5 per cent in Austria to 58.4 per cent in

Japan. Textiles and clothing (excluded from the GSP) are prime examples of developing countries' exports that are discriminated against by systematic import restrictions. Developing countries trade in textiles (30 per cent of their manufactured exports) has been regulated since 1962 under a series of Long-Term Arrangements (LTA) under GATT. Originally, the intention was to assist importing developed countries to adjust to changes in the pattern of world trade in cotton textiles and to provide for an orderly expansion of such trade. In practice the LTA has been used by the developed countries as the basis for a system of detailed controls to cushion the impact on declining textiles industries. Contrary to the undertakings accepted under the LTA there was no significant relaxation of quantitative restrictions on textile imports from the Third World. Instead, voluntary export restrictions were often imposed on some LDCs. In 1974 the Agreement was renewed and became known as the Multi-Fibre Agreement (MFA) with the inclusion of wool and man-made fibres. The MFA provides for a minimum growth rate of textile imports of 6 per cent per annum into the developed countries. But even this is proving too much for beleagured textile industries in these countries. For instance, in the U.K. cotton textile imports now account for 60 per cent of domestic consumption; and in the last fifteen years more than half British cotton workers have lost their jobs. The E.E.C. has agreed to a burden-sharing formula in connection with the new MFA designed to distribute the growth in Community quotas. But it does little to improve market prospects for LDC textile exporters. What little it does threatens to be further restricted by the E.E.C.'s negotiating attitude at the GATT textile committee on the renewal of the MFA which expires in December 1977. The E.E.C. insists that the new protocol incorporates provisions for 'reasonable departures' from the agreement in the form of bilateral accords. This is resisted by LDC textile exporters such as Brazil and India on the ground that the agreement is restrictive enough as it stands. The E.E.C. Commission, at the prodding of the United Kingdom and France, further antagonised LDC exporters by imposing new curbs on textile imports into the Community as from July 1977. The Commission argues that such action was necessary to avoid the loss of 1.6 million jobs in the E.E.C. between 1977 and 1982. During the period 1972–5, the Community absorbed 72 per cent of the total growth of textile imports into the industrialised countries. The U.S. government is also under pressure to take restrictive action on textile imports. Protectionists point to the fact that textiles imports accounted for $3 billion of the total U.S. trade deficit of $9.6 billion in 1976.

Whether it is traditional manufactures such as textiles or newer lines such as electronics, LDC manufactured exports depend on the availability of cheap labour and easily accessible technology. These imports threaten the livelihood of workers in the developed countries. In particular, it is the worst off who are the most affected. A list of U.S. (or E.E.C.) industries with the lowest average earnings corresponds very closely with a list of industries threatened by manufactures from the Third World. Hence, it is quite obvious why the structure of effective protection (effective tariffs and quota protection) of manufacturing industries in the developed countries is significantly and positively correlated with their comparative disadvantage. Protection postpones the need for adjustment. Indeed, current experiments with adjustment assistance in developed countries merely encourage the retention of industries subject to intensive competitive pressure. Despite any accommodating structural changes in the developed countries a few LDCs have experienced a rapid growth of manufactured exports in the decade 1961–71 at an annual rate of 4 per cent higher than that of the industrial countries. In the E.E.C. during the period 1967–9 imports of manufactures and semi-manufactures from the LDCs grew at an annual rate of 24 per cent. Underlying comparative advantage will out; but developed countries' protectionism checks the manufacturing potential of the Third World. The prospects for manufactured exports from developing countries are, however, not entirely bleak. Opportunities are available through (*a*) international sub-contracting by multinational corporations and (*b*) regional integration among developing countries. In the case of both these options for generating exports the LDCs can reap great benefits if they pursue liberal trade and investment policies. The Tokyo Round presents an ideal opportunity for these countries to demonstrate their willingness to practise what they preach.

2.2 Commodity Problems

Traditionally, developing countries have seen their commodity problems as stemming from two pervasive influences in international trade inimical to their development: (*a*) the short-term instability of markets for primary products, reflected in wide year-to-year fluctuations in prices and export earnings and (*b*) the adverse long-term trend in commodity markets, reflected in a tendency for primary products prices to decline relative to prices of manufactured goods resulting in deteriorating terms of trade and sluggish growth in export earnings for commodity-producing countries *v.* industrial countries. From the perspective of the developing countries, heavily dependent on primary product exports, these trends in the operation of international markets for primary commodities are patently unsatisfactory.

With the creation in 1964 of an international forum for the trade grievances of the LDCs in UNCTAD this dissatisfaction with past and existing market forces led to the call for 'a new trade policy for development' – in the commodity sector, for international commodity agreements designed to stabilise prices at 'remunerative' levels and for compensation schemes to protect LDCs against adverse movements in their terms of trade. Recently, inspired by the dazzling success of OPEC in redistributing world income and wealth, the less developed countries renewed their call for 'a new international economic order' (NIEO)[9] to be achieved through comprehensive negotiations with the rich countries on a wide variety of matters affecting their growth prospects. Of all the elements included in the NIEO the commodity problem has attracted the greatest attention and has been the main subject of discussion at the various meetings of the Conference on International Economic Co-operation (the North–South Conference)[10] – specifically UNCTAD IV 'integrated programme' for commodity agreements (including buffer stocks and a common fund for financing them). Before critically examining the 'integrated programme' for commodities it is as well to sort out the issues that provide the basis for LDC complaints in commodity trade.

Primary product exports are the main source of foreign exchange earnings for the majority of LDCs – 50 per cent of the exports of LDCs are primary products, other than fuels. Until the price explosion of 1973–4 primary commodities (excluding oil) had been the least dynamic sector of world trade. During the 1960s exports of primary commodities increased only half as fast as exports of manufactured goods and the share of these commodities in world trade declined from one-third in 1960 to less than a quarter in 1972. Low-income elasticity of demand works against primary producing countries. The income elasticity of demand for foodstuffs has been estimated at 0.6 and for agricultural raw materials 0.5, whereas for manufactures it is 1.9. This lagging growth, accompanied by declining prices, was especially adverse to developing countries heavily dependent on commodity exports. As mentioned above, primary product exports are the main source of foreign exchange earnings for the majority of LDCs and many of these countries are dependent on only one or two primary commodities for the bulk of their exports. This means that their total foreign exchange earnings are very vulnerable to market fluctuations in specific products. Nearly half of the LDCs earn over 50 per cent of their export receipts from a single primary commodity, e.g. coffee, cocoa. About 75 per cent of these countries earn 60 per cent of their receipts from three primary products. However, the developed countries are, in fact, absolutely larger producers of primary commodities than LDCs. In 1970–2 the developing countries accounted for only 47 per cent of world exports of primary products, other than oil. Whatever credence may be attached to the doctrine of declining relative prices for primary products it cannot be regarded as a phenomenon uniquely describing the terms of trade between rich and poor countries.

On the specific allegations about instability and secularly deteriorating terms of trade much has been written. Briefly, the evidence substantiates the existence of short-run instability in primary product prices, but is ambiguous on the adverse terms of trade question. Several studies have confirmed that LDCs are subject to much greater instability in their export earnings than are industrial countries. Whatever index is used to measure instability, the result is the same. MacBean,[11] who analysed the experience of the 1950s, found that the average export instability for LDCs was 3 per cent higher than that for developed countries. For the 1960s other researchers found LDC instability 117 per cent greater than advanced countries instability.[12]

In the last few years the wide price fluctuations experienced in primary commodities have amply demonstrated the instability of world commodity markets. In nominal terms the price index for primary products (excluding oil) rose by 60 per cent during 1973. Between 1973 and 1975 it fell 40 per cent, but rose subsequently by something like 80 per cent during the course of 1976 and early 1977. The commodity cycle is closely associated with fluctuations in the level of output and demand in the industrial countries (allowing for a 4–5-month lag). Speculative purchases, reacting to exchange-rate uncertainty and inflationary expectations, also play a part. The price fluctuations, however, tend to be of greater amplitude than the swings in demand because of the relatively low price elasticity of both demand and supply for most primary commodities. It might be thought that fluctuations in export prices and earnings would inhibit economic growth in LDCs through their impact on investment plans, domestic incomes, savings, tax revenues and above all their capacity to import. However, extensive investigation has failed to detect any retarding effect on economic growth of export instability in primary products.[13]

Export price fluctuations tend to be reflected in unstable export proceeds because of the short-run price inelasticity of demand and supply. Export revenue instability, in turn, leads to abrupt changes in imports. Fiscal revenue and government spending are disrupted by these short-run unpredictable fluctuations, for in the majority of LDCs governments rely heavily on tariffs and other taxes on traded commodities mainly on account of administrative convenience and political expediency. Many LDCs suffer from a perennial 'foreign exchange gap', so that export earnings shortfalls inevitably mean shortages of imported capital goods. Development programmes and other private investment projects are adversely affected with retarding effects on the growth of GNP (gross national product). Investment planning is further complicated by the uncertainty created by price or revenue instability. The rate of return on new investment is reduced because of the increase in the risk element in project evaluation.

What about the second problem – the alleged secular deterioration in LDC terms of trade? It is all too easy to generalise about an inexorable tendency towards adverse terms of trade from the experience of a particular period or sub-set of commodities. For instance, when the existence of the trend was popularised by Prebisch and UNCTAD I in the 1960s it was against the background of a decade of sliding raw materials prices following the Korean War boom; and the notion was given some plausibility. During the decade 1955–65 prices of poor countries' exports fell 6 per cent while the prices of developed countries' exports increased by 8 per cent. However, researchers have failed to detect, over the long run, any such general tendency in respect of all primary commodities. The commodity or net barter terms of trade is an index of export prices, Px, relative to an index of import prices, Pm, i.e. Px/Pm. To determine the changes in a country's terms of trade over a period of time a comparison is made between the latest period, $t = 1$, and an earlier or base period, $t = o$. The terms of trade expressed in terms of the base period is then defined as

$$\frac{Px_1/Px_0}{Pm_1/Pm_0}$$

There are at least four different concepts of the terms of trade; but the one most commonly used in policy discussion and empirical work is the commodity terms of trade. Since the terms of trade is a ratio between two indexes, the results depend on the base period chosen and the items included. In general the results will vary depending on the commodities included in the indexes, the weighting system adopted (i.e. whether the set of weights are those of the base period as in the Laspeyres index, P_1Q_0/P_0Q_0, or of the current period as in the Paasche index, P_1Q_1/P_0Q_1), the countries selected and the time period used. In any case changes in a country's terms of trade do not necessarily accurately measure changes in its economic welfare or gains from trade. The closest the empirical measurement of the terms of trade comes to the notion of national gains from trade is through the index known as the 'single factoral terms of trade'. This measure corrects the commodity terms of trade by an appropriate productivity index to reflect changes in total factor productivity in the export sector. The world price of a country's exports may be falling relative to its import prices, but if this fall in export prices reflects productivity gains then the country may be getting more in exchange (i.e. imports) per unit of factor-service devoted to export production. Looking at the conditions of real resource exchange the country clearly gains in such a situation even though the commodity terms of trade index would show a deterioration. The various terms of trade indexes commonly in use ordinarily refer to commodity trade. Trade in invisibles (e.g. shipping, banking, insurance, tourism), unilateral transactions and changes in the real value of foreign exchange reserves resulting from price alterations are excluded. Changes in the quality of exports and imports are not reflected in the indexes. The same is true of transport costs in relation to exports, since by convention exports are measured at f.o.b. prices (i.e. excluding cost of transport) whereas imports are valued c.i.f. (i.e. including transport charges).

Evidence on the terms of trade is difficult to interpret especially when used for policy purposes such as a reform of international commodity markets to rig the terms of trade in favour of developing countries. The fact is that there are wide divergencies in market structures and earnings trends for individual commodities. For instance, in the decade 1962–72 commodity export earnings for LDCs increased at an annual rate of only 4.3 per cent. But exports of six commodities – copper, iron-ore, timber, sugar, beef and bananas – accounting for 40 per cent of their total export earnings, grew at a rate of 7.8 per cent. During the same period the prices of primary commodities exhibited the same highly divergent trends. While agricultural raw materials prices declined substantially relative to the prices of manufactured goods, the prices of foodstuffs and metals actually increased.

Turning now to the UNCTAD programme for commodities (generally known as the Corea Plan, after UNCTAD's Secretary-General Gamani Corea), the central feature is the establishment of a series of international buffer stocks for the main export commodities of the LDCs starting with ten 'core' commodities (coffee, cocoa, copper, cotton, jute, rubber, sisal, sugar, tea and tin) and the creation of a Common Fund for financing the stocks. Additional proposals call for the expansion of the processing of primary commodities in developing countries, improved market access for LDC exports of primary and processed products and improved compensatory financing for the maintenance of stability in export earnings. The Common Fund – the only really integrative feature – is crucial to the whole policy. The Fund will lend financial resources to individual commodity agencies for the acquisition and maintenance of adequate stocks of the ten core commodities – the amount to be repaid when commodity agencies acquire funds from the disposal of stocks. In this way the Fund, acting as a financial link between the commodity agencies, will be self-financing. The estimated total requirement is $6000m., half of which will be needed immediately to get the commodity schemes off the ground. The financial resources will be raised in the form of capital contributions and loans to be provided by exporting and importing countries, OPEC, multilateral financing agencies and borrowing in the private capital market. Although separate agreements would have to be negotiated for each commodity, two advantages are claimed for a common source of finance. First, the Common Fund would need less finance than the aggregate of the individual stocking schemes because of the different pattern and timing of fluctuations in the various commodity markets. Second, because of the economies of finance, risks can be pooled, the safety of lenders enhanced and borrowing costs made correspondingly smaller.

The objective of commodity agreements according to the UNCTAD programme is to reduce short-term fluctuations in the prices of primary commodities exported by developing countries. The manager of each buffer stock, armed with financial resources from the Common Fund, will endeavour to maintain the commodity price within a specified range by purchases and sales in the international market. Buffer stocks can, indeed, if backed by sufficient funds and are skilfully managed, reduce the volatility in commodity prices. Success depends on the level at which the price range is set. This requires accurate forecasting of price trends and frequent re-examination of the price range in the light of current and forecast trends. Buffer-stock financing could be exhausted by a protracted price decline that was not fully anticipated, as happened in the tin agreement at least four times since 1956 when the present agreement came into force. Those were periods of excess supply when the floor price had to be protected through the imposition of export quotas on producer members. At other times the opposite situation prevailed – the buffer's tin stocks ran out as the market price rose above the ceiling. This was the case for several months in 1977 when the price of tin averaged 10 per cent above the ceiling set by the International Tin Council. Over the years the maximum and minimum prices have been progressively raised so as to reflect the trend of market pressures. Not all commodities are suitable for buffer stock stabilisation; commodities must be homogeneous and capable of being stored without deterioration at relatively low cost. Storage and maintenance costs for metals are relatively low (in the range 0.03 per cent to 0.08 per cent of average market value) compared with agricultural raw materials and foodstuffs (around 0.5 per cent of market value). The main costs involved in buffer-stock operations are the capital costs of acquiring and carrying the stock. This is the social opportunity cost (or earnings forgone) of tying up capital, and must be set against any social gains from price stabilisation. Although the history of international commodity agreements goes back to the 1920s the record has been one of almost total failure. Besides the day-to-day management problems the major stumbling block has been failure of the participating countries to agree on the objectives of such agreements. The UNCTAD programme has not resolved this problem. The pricing principles for commodity agreements envisaged by the programme are ambiguous, to say the least. Price stabilisation is stated to be the main objective; but 'equitable' and 'remunerative' prices over the long run are also included. Even more controversial was the original proposal for indexing the prices of commodities to prices of manufactured imports of LDCs. This has been seen by the importing countries as an attempt to raise commodity prices above their long-term trend – in other words, to effect resource transfers through higher prices. The concentration on buffer stocks as the main regulatory instrument obscures the relationship between price stabilisation and revenue stabilisation, further adding to the ambiguity over objectives. Price stabilisation does not automatically yield revenue stabilisation. Only in a certain exceptional configuration of supply and demand elasticities will this be the case, i.e. when there is a supply shift in a range where both supply and demand curves are price inelastic. The source of instability is important in determining whether or not price stabilisation is likely to bring about revenue stabilisation; and within the constraints imposed by market characteristics of particular commodities, priorities must be agreed accordingly. For instance, LDCs must decide whether commodity stabilisation through buffer stocks is intended to:

(1) stabilise export revenue;
(2) maximise profits and welfare from exports or
(3) minimise export expenditure and maximise welfare of commodity importing countries.

It is not at all obvious that more than one of these targets can be achieved at the same time. If the purpose of stabilisation is to stabilise and increase the taxes that governments of developing countries can extract from their primary producers then revenue stabilisation is appropriate. On the other hand, price stabilisation is helpful in avoiding economic inefficiencies at the microeconomic level; resource allocation decisions can take place on the basis of stable prices rather than being disturbed by erratic economic price signals during boom-and-bust commodity cycles.

In a detailed analysis of commodity price stabilisation and the developing world a World Bank study[14] came to some interesting conclusions. For instance, on the basis of their analysis the authors advise that if price stabilisation is intended to maximise income and welfare benefits of the developing countries as producers (exporters) they should choose those commodities whose prices fluctuate mostly as a result of supply shifts. If, on the other hand, the objective is to maximise welfare and minimise import expenditure of developing countries as consumers (importers) they should choose those commodities whose prices fluctuate mainly by demand factors.

Out of a sample of seventeen primary commodities the results indicate that LDCs, as exporters, would benefit from price stabilisation in only two commodities: coffee and cocoa. As importers, LDCs would benefit from price stabilisation only in wheat. Commodities whose prices are volatile mainly due to demand shifts – most minerals, metals and rubber – are poor candidates for price stabilisation if the objective is to maximise the income and welfare of exporting countries, although it is possible to stabilise export revenue. On the distribution of income and welfare gains from international price stabilisation, three further conclusions emerged:

(1) LDCs are likely to derive only modest benefits from commodity agreement. Coffee and cocoa, where clear gains are likely from price stabilisation, account for only 17 per cent of LDC export earnings; and wheat (where LDCs can benefit from stabilisation as importers) comprises about 15 per cent of total import expenditures by LDCs.

(2) International price stabilisation of minerals and metals would benefit primarily the developed countries (as the largest importers and consumers).

(3) In the two commodities (coffee and cocoa) where the LDCs stand to benefit as exporters from price stabilisation the simultaneous achievement of price and revenue stabilisation does not depend crucially on the existence of a buffer stock – both the demand for and supply of these commodities being price inelastic in the short run.

These World Bank findings lend support to the criticism that the UNCTAD commodities programme is over-ambitious. The developed countries will have to underwrite the largest part of a programme of dubious value both in terms of its functioning and its effects on the development process. Experience shows that international commodity agreements are an exceedingly doubtful instrument for promoting economic development. Economic theory suggests that direct transfers are a more efficient means than price supports for transferring income from consumers to sellers (as, for instance, deficiency payments in domestic agricultural programmes). What this implies is that greater emphasis should be put on compensatory financing arrangements, if not as a substitute for commodity stabilisation schemes, then as a valuable complement. Indeed, improved compensatory financing facilities figure in the UNCTAD integrated programme; but the international discussion has so far been dominated by commodity agreements as stabilising instruments. If the objective is to alleviate the economic difficulties caused by export revenue fluctuations (for instance, if a country's exports suffer from a poor crop) then the export earnings stabilisation schemes of the IMF (in operation since 1963) or those of the E.E.C.'s Lomé Convention are the appropriate instruments. These schemes provide compensatory financing related to shortfalls of foreign exchange earnings in relation to expected levels. The Lomé Convention (1975) between the E.E.C. and forty-nine—soon to be fifty-two—developing countries incorporates a commodity scheme (STABEX) which seeks to protect ACP exporters (African, Caribbean and Pacific countries) against fluctuations in export proceeds by assuring financial transfers to them when their effective earnings from one year's exports to the E.E.C. fall below a specified level (the average value in the four preceding years). The first transfers under STABEX were made in July 1976: eighteen ACP countries, thirteen of which are among the poorest, benefited from this insurance against losses incurred in 1975. The IMF compensatory financing facility has been of great assistance to developing countries, especially since it was liberalised in December 1975. Drawings soared to $2.7 billions in 1976, compared with a peak of $350m. in 1972. The setting up of a comprehensive system for the stabilisation of export revenues deserves greater attention within the context of the integrated programme, especially if they are tied to national development plans to ensure progress in adjustment of the economies. The potential benefits from such a comprehensive system would meet with general approval in the industrial countries and would induce them to make the necessary financial contributions.

Another element of the integrated programme that will command wide support is the call for increased processing of raw materials in developing countries. The processing of raw materials often accounts for a large proportion of the value of the material itself as reflected in the wide differential between the market price of the finished commodity and the price received by the raw material producer. Local raw-material processing through vertical diversification would enable LDC producers to appropriate this value added and contribute to higher employment and export earnings. According to some estimates developing countries at present receive only 15 per cent of the final selling price of their produce.[15] Although well suited to the resource base of developing countries in other respects, some processing activities, e.g. minerals industries require large capital investments and skilled labour inputs. In such cases the expansion of processing industries in the Third World would be retarded without the greater involvement of private enterprise from the developed world. Just as important is the reduction in tariff escalation on processed goods in developed countries. Diversification, both vertically and horizontally, is the surest way to escape at once from export price instability and sluggish export earnings. It is, in fact, the essence of the development process which consists of exploring alternative income-producing opportunities, moving into lines of production with more favourable market prospects which increase the productivity of a country's land, labour and capital resources.

As indicated earlier, there has been much criticism in the industrial countries of UNCTAD's integrated programme for commodities. The criticism has been less of the ends than of the means envisaged by the programme. And this has been reflected in the several UN meetings on the subject. A negotiating conference on the programme between LDCs and the developed countries in April 1977 broke up without reaching agreement. The sticking point was the Common Fund. The United States, backed by Japan, Canada and Australia, opposed the principle of a common fund; and, while the E.E.C. is committed to the idea, some E.E.C. members prefer instead a general system of compensatory credit or financing on the lines discussed earlier. Even among the developing countries some differences arose as to the objectives of the Common Fund. A proposal by African countries that the Common Fund should be used to promote raw-material processing and diversification generally in the Third World was effectively blocked by Latin American countries, which stand to gain most from the proposed buffer stocks. As a major raw-material producer with an interest in price stability the United States is likely to abandon its opposition to the Common Fund. Despite disagreements between the rich and poor countries over the modalities of the integrated programme and the NIEO the differences seem likely to narrow as political opinion in the developed countries comes to realise the potentialities for world economic recovery of sustaining export earnings, income and growth in the Third World. As a matter of practical self-interest there are mutual benefits to be gained from co-operation on a more coherent development strategy to help poor countries realise their aspirations. The well-being of the developed and developing countries are bound up together in an increasingly interdependent system. This was publicly recognised by the leaders of the seven industrial countries at their May 1977 summit meeting in London.

2.3   LDC Debts

The developing countries incurred huge external debts during 1974–6. In two years the total indebtedness of LDCs jumped from $80,000m. in 1973 to $120,000m. in 1975 (an increase of 50 per cent). It was around $180,000m. in 1976, or more than twice the level of 1973. Estimates of the size of some LDC debts in 1975 are shown in Table 2.5. This rapid build up of LDC debt has prompted fears of defaults on the massive loans they have received, imperilling both the banking system in the developed world and the financial stability and creditworthiness of LDCs. These fears were heightened by demands both at UNCTAD IV and at the North–South Conference for a moratorium on official debt and a rescheduling of private debts over twenty-five years. In banking circles there was much talk of credit running out for 'bad risk' countries; that the burden of debt and of debt service would be too great for developing countries to carry. However, such fears are largely unfounded – so far only Zaïre has actually defaulted on a major loan. Some of the more developed Third World countries, such as Mexico and Brazil, which rely heavily on

Table 2.5

Estimated External Debts of Selected non-OPEC LDCs, end 1975 (data in $ billions)

	Total*	Public sector only†	Liabilities to commercial banks
Brazil	21.9	10.8	14.8
Mexico	19.0	9.7	13.5
Argentina	7.3	3.5	3.2
Chile	5.2	4.5	0.8
Peru	4.5	3.1	2.3
Colombia	3.7	2.5	1.6
South Korea	7.6	5.2	3.3
Taiwan	4.7	3.2	2.1
Turkey	4.5	3.4	1.0
Philippines	3.8	1.5	2.0
Thailand	1.8	0.6	1.2
Zaïre	1.5	1.3	0.8

* Estimated outstanding disbursed external debt of public and private sectors: individual country data are not entirely comparable; some countries do not report all external debt of the private sector.

† Outstanding disbursed external debt of public sector, including private sector debt guaranteed by public sector and use of IMF credit, with original maturity of more than one year.

Sources: World Financial Markets (Sept 1976) Morgan Guaranty Trust, New York; World Bank, *World Debt Tables* (EC–167/76) and *Borrowing in International Capital Markets* (EC–181).

world financial markets for development capital, are anxious not to impair their credit ratings and have emphasised their intentions to continue servicing the debts. The steep increase in LDC indebtedness arose from a combination of circumscribed events in the world economy during 1974–5; and already the indications are that normal patterns are being restored. Nevertheless, the extent of LDC indebtedness, especially in the case of the poorest LDCs, requires careful international monitoring and more prudent balance of payments management on the part of such LDCs.

The problem of LDC debts is nothing new; what is new is the sudden large increase in new debt commitments and the correspondingly large burden of debt service. During the decade of the 1960s the medium- and long-term external public debt of LDCs grew at an annual rate of 14 per cent. Debt-service payments (including both interest and amortisation) rose at 15.7 per cent per annum. Even in those days this created difficulties for some countries; eleven countries asked for debt-relief in the form of rescheduling or stretchout of debt-service payments. Much of the transfer of resources to developing countries was closely related to the so-called 'development deficit' of LDCs – the difference between their domestic savings and investment. Foreign capital imports supplement internally generated savings or foreign exchange availability. Throughout the 1960s the difference between savings and investment remained stable at about 2 per cent of their collective GNP; and transfers of real resources from the rest of the world enabled LDCs to sustain an average growth rate of 5 per cent per annum. From 1971 to 1974 the *per capita* growth rate of the non-oil LDCs averaged $2\frac{1}{2}$ per cent per annum.

A decade of steady economic progress was abruptly halted by the convulsions in the world economy during 1974–5, i.e. the quadrupling of oil prices and the recession in the industrial world. The oil price rise resulted in a $10.000m. increase in the total import bill of LDCs in both 1974 and 1975; and the recession in the developed countries towards the end of 1974 slowed the rise in their export earnings. In the face of these threats to their continued economic development the developing countries attempted to cushion the fall of investment and consumption. The level of imports was maintained in many countries through offsetting expansion of the domestic monetary base and subsidies. From 1973 there was a massive deterioration of their current account balance of payments. The LDCs could have financed part of this deficit by drawing upon their reserves accumulated in the fat years of the early 1970s (estimated to have increased by $8000m. in 1973). But, in aggregate, their reserves showed little net change. Instead, they borrowed. In the absence of this inflow of external resources standards of living and long-term development programmes could not have been maintained. By this policy response – the efforts of these countries to maintain their imports through borrowing – the developing countries supported world economic activity, particularly the production of investment goods.

To that extent it had a significant positive effect on exports and growth in the industrial countries. According to Common Market sources, had the developing countries cut back on their imports to avoid piling up deficits, the consequence to the E.E.C. would have been an additional 3 million unemployed.[16]

In 1974 the LDCs borrowed $36,330m. abroad, about half of it from private lenders (bond issues as well as bank loans). Borrowings increased again in 1975 and 1976 to bring the total outstanding external debt of non-oil LDCs to around $180,000m. compared with $83,000m. in 1973. It was this acceleration in the growth rate of outstanding debt, together with the changing structure of that debt, that gave cause for concern. The growth in the relative importance of private bank lending to LDCs has affected the structure of their external debt. Borrowing from private sources requires repayment in shorter time periods (typically five to seven years) also at higher rates of interest. The shortening of the average maturity of a country's debt bearing high-interest charges means that the ratio of the future debt service to the debt outstanding as of some base period increases accordingly. Debt-service time ratios calculated for developing countries during the period 1969–74 show a significant increase.[17] This indicates hardening of borrowing terms mainly because of the increased level of international interest rates in the 1970s and the relative growth in private source borrowing. The structure of developing countries' debt is such that during the next three to five years, payments of interest and principal will escalate sharply. This requires careful debt-management policies on the part of those LDCs (Latin American, advanced Mediterranean and East Asian countries) that borrowed heavily from private financial institutions. In many LDCs the cost of servicing the external debt exceeds 20 per cent of their export earnings. Unless export earnings pick up rapidly some of these countries would require additional net capital inflows to service the debts contracted in 1974–6. As the experience of 1974–5 shows, the developing countries are reluctant to curtail the growth of imports; and this is because imports, especially of investment goods, must rise if economic growth is to be sustained. A reduction in the capacity to import will tend to reduce the rate of investment. It may also reduce the utilisation of existing capacity as imported raw materials and intermediate inputs become scarce. But the capacity to import is determined by the rate of growth of foreign exchange earnings, particularly from exports. With a high ratio of debt-service payments to export earnings (usually called the debt-service ratio) a country's development programme must generate a growing excess of foreign exchange earnings over import costs to allow the country to meet its debt-service payments. Additionally, when debt-service payments are growing rapidly as at present, foreign exchange earnings must rise at least as rapidly as the rate of growth of debt repayments if the capacity to import is not to be seriously impaired. Short-run fluctuations in export earnings take on a more ominous aspect when a country's debt-service ratio is high, since a given percentage drop in export earnings causes a larger percentage reduction in the all-important capacity to import. On top of this, an element of uncertainty surrounds the forecasting of LDC balance of payments owing to the fact that over half of the loans from private institutions carry variable interest charges. One recompense is that, as large debtors, LDCs enjoy an advantage from continued world inflation – it reduces the burden, in real terms, of servicing their existing debt. Indeed, to a large extent, the rapid growth of LDC debt since 1972 reflects the high rates of inflation in the world economy. It is therefore important to distinguish the real from the nominal burden of the debt when considering the question of whether or not the LDCs have incurred excessive external debts in recent years. The way to do this is to deflate the external financial debt of these countries by changes in the dollar prices of either their aggregate exports or imports. During the period 1972–6, when the LDC total debt accelerated sharply, the import and export prices of these countries both doubled so that the real debt of the LDCs as a group increased by only 20 per cent over the period.

In the same way, increases in debt-service ratios can be misleading as measures of debt burden if they are not presented on a price-adjusted basis. Although the situation obviously differs from country to country, the aggregate debt burden of the LDCs appears to have increased much less rapidly than their nominal debt. The evaluation of debt-servicing capacity (and, hence, the identification of countries likely to default or require reschedulings) requires more information than that provided by financial ratio analysis. For instance, one would need to consider for any particular country: (1) the size of export earnings; (2) the growth of real GNP; (3) the level of domestic savings; (4) the dependence on imported goods (including the ratio of imports to GNP and the ratio of 'essential imports' to total imports); (5) the projected growth rate of exports; (6) the international liquidity position of the country, i.e. the ratio of gross international reserves to imports of goods and services. These factors bear directly or indirectly on the course of the balance of payments. In the short run the state of the balance of payments is crucially important in the determination of debt-servicing capacity. A country can incur a large external debt and sustain a high debt-service ratio so long as its balance of payments is in a healthy state. On the other hand a country with a much lower debt-service ratio can find itself in difficulty to the extent that debt rescheduling becomes necessary if it incurs large payments deficits. But, ultimately, the question as to whether or not a particular country has over-extended itself by incurring excessive debt can only be resolved by relating the productivity of the additional investments financed by foreign borrowing to the cost (or interest-rate charges) of such external capital. If the increase in productivity is greater than the interest and amortisation charges on the loan, net real national income increases and foreign borrowing is justified. Bearing in mind the fact that developing countries as a group have an impressive growth record – 6 per cent annually in the 1960s and 5 per cent since 1974 – one is inclined to conclude that capital has been flowing in the right direction towards the LDCs, and that these countries have not borrowed too much from abroad. Looking at the most recent years, i.e. 1972–6, the real GNP of the less-developed countries rose by 20 per cent. This is about the same rate as the increase in their real debt over this period.[18]

Despite earlier fears the prospects appear favourable for the resolution of LDC debt problems. There was a drop in the level of borrowing from $4200m. in the final quarter of 1976 to $2200m. in the first quarter of 1977. Both foreign exchange reserves and some commodity prices increased, e.g. coffee, which allowed some countries to reduce new borrowing commitments. The likelihood of widespread rescheduling or defaults on LDC debt is moreover diminished by government guarantees in the lending countries and the claims that the LDCs have on international agencies, in particular the IMF. In April 1977 the IMF proposed a new $10,000m. financing facility for countries in the Third World suffering from acute balance of payments problems accentuated by recent events.

Further Reading

A. K. Bhattacharya, *Foreign Trade and International Development* (Lexington Mass.: Lexington Books, 1976). An up-to-date discussion of LDC trade problems.

G. K. Helleiner, *International Trade and Economic Development* (Harmondsworth: Penguin Books, 1972). This text describes and analyses the issues of world trade as they relate to the LDCs.

K. Morton and P. Tulloch, *Trade and Developing Countries* (London: Croom Helm–ODI, 1977).

T. Murray, *Trade Preferences for Developing Countries* (London: Macmillan, 1977). A detailed, critical analysis of the GSP scheme.

B. Södersten, *International Economics* (London: Macmillan, 1971). Chap. 23 contains a useful, clear exposition of the trade problems of developing countries.

P. Streeten (ed.), *Trade Strategies for Development*, Papers of the 9th Cambridge Conference on Development Problems (London: Macmillan, 1973).

CHAPTER 3

East–West Trade

3.1 The Background

Conventionally, 'East–West Trade' is concerned with the commercial relations between the socialist centrally-planned economies of Eastern Europe (the Soviet Union, Bulgaria, Czechoslovakia, East Germany, Hungary, Poland and Romania) and the industrial market economies of the West. It is well known that political factors have dominated (and severely limited) post-war East–West commerce; hence the saying, 'East–West business depends on East–West politics.' Now that the United States has concluded a trade agreement with the Soviet Union (1972) the political climate for expanded East–West trade has never been better. Consequently, one imagines, economic factors will bear more importantly on the situation. Indeed, it is well known that basic economic pressures have been behind the latest Soviet and East European (E.E.) moves towards expanded Western contacts. At the same time Western firms, aided by the easing of official restrictions, are finding new ways of doing business with the East.

In this chapter we take a fresh look at the economic factors underlying East–West trade. In particular we focus on the economic influences shaping the volume, composition and direction of East European trade with the West. First, the background.

E.E. countries conduct their foreign trade on a different basis from that ordinarily followed in the West. In the West decisions to import and export are made largely by profit-seeking competitive enterprises on the basis of relative prices in domestic and foreign markets. The E.E. countries on the other hand, being centrally planned economies, engage in state trading. Traditionally, at any rate, foreign trade in an E.E.

country is a state monopoly directed by the ministry of foreign trade and conducted through central agencies known as foreign trade corporations (FTCs). This system of trading ensures that trade flows conform to plans and planning requirements rather than being guided by current relative prices. In any case, prices in the typical E.E. country do not necessarily reflect market conditions; moreover, these domestic prices are largely insulated from external influences, and the official exchange rate is largely redundant. However, since the mid-1960s as part of the package of reform measures all the E.E. countries, including the Soviet Union, have taken steps to improve the efficiency of foreign trade management by decentralising decision-making and by allowing domestic prices to reflect factor costs, including a more realistic valuation of traded inputs. Although the extent to which market forces and competitive influences have been allowed to alter traditional foreign trade, conduct varies from country to country, the general picture is one of greater freedom for producing enterprises to engage directly in import and export transactions, a reduction in the number of compulsory annual plan targets for trade, and the use of more realistic substitutes, e.g. shadow exchange rates or 'foreign trade multipliers', as they are called, for the generally overvalued official exchange rates. Hungary has gone the furthest in liberalising foreign trade since the inauguration in 1968 of its reform programme. Although in the last four years the Hungarians have faced serious problems of economic management arising from greater exposure to rapid world market changes, e.g. the need to resort to frequent *ad hoc* interventions such as the use of taxes and subsidies to maintain price stability and shield enterprises from external economic fluctuations, the planners have not retreated from the liberalisation policy.

The foreign trade of the E.E. countries is also strongly influenced by their mutual ties within COMECON – the East European 'common market'. Set up by Stalin in 1949, COMECON,[1] or, to give it its full title, the Council for Mutual Economic Assistance, served as the economic mechanism for consolidating Soviet hegemony in Eastern Europe. Ostensibly announced as a riposte to America's massive effort to reconstruct the war-shattered economies of Western Europe, Stalin saw it developing into the nucleus of a 'second world market' independent of, and rivalling, the moribund capitalist world market. For a time, under the pressures of the Cold War and their own gigantic industrialisation drive, the COMECON countries seemed set on a course that could eventually lead to the realisation of Stalin's dream. They diverted trade towards each other and away from their traditional Western partners. When COMECON was set up no member carried on more than 30 per cent of its trade with the others. Five years later, trade among themselves reached a peak of 73 per cent. This mutual trade intensity was largely accounted for by a flourishing trade in machinery, equipment and industrial raw materials which reflected the rapid build-up of industrial capacity in each country. But since the national industrialisation efforts were planned on the basis of import-substitution policies, they all developed very similar industrial structures. They were all trying to sell basically the same types of machinery and equipment to each other and scrambling among themselves for the region's (in effect, the Soviet Union's) supply of raw materials. At first the more industrialised members — Czechoslovakia and East Germany — found a ready market in the region for their exports of machinery; but as import-substitution industrial production got into stride in the less-developed member countries, surplus industrial capacity became evident almost everywhere. In addition, because of lack of competition from Western producers, enterprises in Czechoslovakia and East Germany failed to keep abreast of technological developments both in production and marketing. While it became more difficult to sell machinery within the COMECON area, Western markets were even more difficult to penetrate because of inferior quality and poor marketing. Countries like Hungary, Romania and Poland showed an increasing preference for modern Western machinery and consumer goods.

In the early 1960s the shortcomings of COMECON became quite evident to the economic managers of these countries. They had diverted trade towards each other, but had hardly created any new trade among themselves. The outspoken nationalism of some COMECON member states, e.g. Romania, and the common strategy of 'extensive' development prevented the creation of supranational agencies designed to exploit cost advantages and scale economies in locating new productive capacity. It was the manifest unprofitability of much of intra-COMECON trade that led to the renewal of links with the 'capitalist world market'. Intra-COMECON trade fell from the very high level reached in the 1950s, but still averages two-thirds of the total trade of member countries. The Western European countries, in particular among the developed countries, responded in positive ways to the obvious desire of the more trade-orientated COMECON countries (Hungary, Poland and Romania) for mutual exchanges. The West European countries adopted liberal trade policies towards the East, including reductions in the list of embargoed goods and easier credits. The United States, until 1971, maintained a much stricter control on exports to the COMECON area; as a result, most of the increase in business with Eastern Europe during the 1960s went to Western European countries.[2] The easing of American restrictions on East—West trade and the initiatives taken by the United States in 1971 and 1972 to reach a trade agreement with the Soviet Union were partly designed to put American exporters on an even footing with West European competitors. Unfortunately for some American businessmen, U.S. Export—Import Bank credit facilities for export to the Soviet Union were withdrawn in January 1975 after being in operation for only two years following the Congressional debate on human rights in the Soviet Union and freedom of emigration. It has been estimated that this action cost U.S. business between $1000m. and $2000m. of lost orders during the years 1975—6.[3] This restriction is likely to be lifted by the Carter Administration as part of its announced 'new beginning' in East—West relations.

Given that the level of trade was artificially restricted in the previous decade it is not surprising that the 1960s saw a rapid increase in the rate of growth of East—West trade. E.E. imports from developed countries rose at an average annual rate of 12 per cent; E.E. exports to developed countries averaged 10 per cent per annum. See Tables 3.1 and 3.2 for recent data on East—West trade. East—West trade expanded more rapidly than intra-COMECON trade and world trade in general. This expansion continued into the early 1970s. East—West trade is

Table 3.1

Trade of Industrial Western Countries with COMECON, 1975

| | Exports | | Imports | |
	$ millions	Percentage change over 1974	$ millions	Percentage change over 1974
West Germany	8051	16	4568	7
Italy	2175	32	1920	2
Yugoslavia	1871	29	1843	9
France	2597	61	1693	28
Finland	1317	47	1571	4
United Kingdom	1292	29	1514	− 5
Sweden	1096	40	1089	30
Austria	1280	18	955	9
Netherlands	797	5	790	21
Belgium	858	3	620	8
Denmark	306	10	519	22
United States	2787	95	780	− 18
Canada	598	270	162	− 16
Japan	2199	32	1375	− 19

Source: United Nations, *Economic Survey of Europe in 1976*, part I, p. 126 (New York: Economic Commission for Europe, 1977).

Table 3.2

Value of COMECON Countries' Exports to the West, 1975

| | Exports | |
	$ millions	Percentage change over 1974
Bulgaria	458	− 8
Czechoslovakia	1943	7
East Germany	2617	10
Hungary	1360	− 7
Poland	3380	13
Romania	1789	3
Soviet Union	9660	6
Total	21,207	6

Source: UN, *Economic Survey of Europe in 1976*, part I, p. 126.

more important to the E.E. countries than it is to the group of developed Western countries. For the former countries it comprises 25 per cent of their total trade, but it is less than 4 per cent of developed countries' total trade. Romania and Poland have the highest share of exports with the West; the Soviet Union and Bulgaria have the lowest — see Table 3.3.

Table 3.3

East—West Trade as Percentages of Total Trade of COMECON Countries, 1973

	East—West Trade as percentage of Total Trade
Bulgaria	14.6
Czechoslovakia	23.6
East Germany	27.9
Hungary	28.2
Poland	39.8
Romania	41.7
Soviet Union	26.6

Source: IMF and World Bank Group, *Direction of Trade*, various issues.

East—West trade certainly has a growth potential. The E.E. countries produce one-third of the world's industrial output, but account for only 10 per cent of the total trade of East and West. The East European market is large and fairly affluent, comprising 350m. people, with a combined GNP of about $800,000m. *Per capita* GNP in the member states of COMECON exceed the levels reached by most countries of Latin America, Asia and Africa. The latest national five-year plans seek to maintain current growth rates, i.e. around 5 per cent, and to increase the output of consumer goods. Foreign trade plans envisage an aggregate growth of 30–35 per cent up to 1980. To achieve these priorities the E.E. countries must improve the productivity and allocative efficiency of their economies. This is, in fact, the rationale for the economic reforms. A common trend towards declining factor productivity – even in the Soviet Union[4] – over the past decade has been largely responsible for the failure to maintain the earlier high rates of output growth. In the mid-1960s it was realised that something had to be done to improve productivity in the area. No longer can these countries count on large increases in labour and capital inputs to bolster growth rates. Consequently they are shifting from what they call 'extensive' to 'intensive' growth. They aim to modernise their economies and to catch up on American and West European technology. And they are pinning their hopes on expanded trade with the West to speed up this modernisation process. In one degree or another, therefore, COMECON countries are looking to industrial countries' expertise for help in modernising industry, increasing productivity and establishing consumer goods industries. But E.E. aspirations are impeded by limited ability to earn Western convertible currencies – because Western demand for their traditional exports is slow-growing. They depend heavily on exports of food, fuels and crude materials. Such products account for nearly 60 per cent of their exports to Western Europe, for instance; while chemicals, machinery and transport equipment account for some 15 per cent and other manufactured goods for about 25 per cent. On the other hand, about 80 per cent of Western exports to Eastern Europe consists of manufactured goods. The E.E. countries have been accumulating debt. In 1972 Eastern Europe and the Soviet Union were each estimated to have a convertible currency debt with Western Europe of some $2000m. and about the same with other Western countries.[5] Five years later, in 1977, COMECON taken as a bloc and including the borrowings of its two regional banks had run up a debt in the West conservatively estimated in excess of $40,000m. The bulk of the debt consists of medium- and long-term Western credits extended in the last three years to finance purchases of imported plant and equipment. Half of the accumulated debt was incurred by the smaller E.E. countries. However, at least in respect of Soviet oil and gas, the prospects for earning convertible currency have improved considerably in the last few years. The smaller E.E. countries are not so fortunate. Poland, for instance, with an accumulated debt of some $12,000m. finds that in order to service the debt at an annual rate of $2000m it has to allocate something like 30 per cent of its convertible currency earnings. To check the growth of its debt by 1980 Poland would have to achieve an annual growth rate of exports to the West of approximately 28 per cent, as compared with an average of 13 per cent attained in 1975–6. COMECON countries are, however, hopeful that newly completed plants built with Western firms' assistance will provide new export capability and help reduce their deficits.

With this background look into some main features of East–West trade we turn to consider the obstacles that still stand in the way of further expansion of this trade.

3.2　East–West Trade Problems

The recent upsurge in East–West trade has raised expectations among Western businessmen that this trade will expand dynamically in the future. However, while recognising that the ultimate potential for mutually beneficial economic interchange is substantial, it is appropriate to remind ourselves of the inhibiting factors which artificially restrict this trade. There are obstacles both on the Eastern and Western sides which stem from the differences in economic systems. On the Eastern side, the negative factors tending to reduce the volume of East–West trade are:

(1) currency inconvertibility and bilateralism;
(2) insufficient export capacity, and
(3) the substantial economic interdependence in COMECON. On the Western side, the obstacles take the form of import quotas, discriminatory tariff treatment, prohibitive anti-dumping duties and vestiges of the Cold War strategic embargo.

Taking the former set of obstacles first, the most serious is currency inconvertibility and the attendant disadvantages of the Eastern practice of negotiating business by means of bilateral trade agreements. E.E. currencies are almost completely inconvertible. Transactions in Western currencies by E.E. residents are strictly controlled by the authorities. Exchange controls also apply to non-residents. Individuals are not free to sell E.E. currencies for convertible, i.e. Western currencies. Moreover, since domestic currencies are never exchanged for other currencies their exchange rates need not (and do not) function as real prices. It is well known that the rouble and other E.E. currencies are greatly overvalued, i.e. their purchasing power is much less, at the official exchange rates, than that of Western currencies. Of course, because the E.E. exchange rates are out of line with market reality, a black market has developed in the U.S. dollar, the German mark and other Western currencies.

The inconvertibility of E.E. currencies stems from (*a*) balance of payments pressures and a shortage of foreign exchange and (*b*) the need to safeguard the integrity of national plans. The first reason is fairly obvious, and is similar to the situation faced by many developing countries. But, in addition, E.E. countries cannot allow convertibility without disrupting plan targets and suffering unacceptable economic losses. To see this, recall that the E.E. countries all have distorted price structures (prices that differ from real opportunity costs) with intermediate or producer goods being typically low-priced (often below cost) and consumer goods high-priced. In addition, there are wide discrepancies between world market prices and domestic prices for similar goods. If foreigners were allowed to shop around freely in E.E. domestic markets they would buy intermediate goods and sell consumer goods. The resulting transactions, based on these distorted prices, would be quite inefficient from the E.E. point of view and would make planning well nigh impossible.

The E.E. preference for doing business by means of bilateral agreements can be attributed to inconvertibility and the factors behind it. A bilateral trade agreement usually covers periods of two to six years supplemented by more detailed annual trade protocols. The agreement specifies the total volume of trade and the classes of goods to be exported and imported. This method of trading has undoubtedly facilitated economic planning and reduced the need for currency transactions. However justified, the fact remains that bilateralism has limited the volume and character of their trade with the rest of the world. For instance, the volume of imports into Eastern

Europe has tended to be limited to the volume of their exports. Officials in Eastern Europe have for some time recognised the disadvantages of bilateralism, and recently they have tended to move away from the stricter forms of it. The number of bilateral payments agreements has decreased, and they have become less rigid. The bilateralism constraint should be less important in the future on account of a greater willingness on the part of banks and Western governments to provide credit support for exports to the East. In fact, bilateralism is much more the norm among the East Europeans themselves than it is in East–West trade. Only 2–3 per cent of intra-COMECON trade is settled on a multilateral basis, whereas East–West trade appears far more multilateral. This is because the E.E. countries have used foreign exchange earned as surpluses with some countries to offset deficits with others. The Soviet Union has also in the past sold gold to settle current debts in Western countries.

The next trade-restricting factor on the Eastern side is due to insufficient export capacity. This springs from the relative managerial and technological backwardness and unresponsiveness to markets that still plague Eastern production. The range of products is limited; often, as in the case of consumer goods, they are of poor quality and not up to the average Western standards. Marketing and service facilities are not fully developed. The long-range planning as practised in Eastern Europe is not geared to meeting changing Western tastes. Finally, as their exports to the West are heavily concentrated on products for which demand grows relatively slowly the full potential dynamism of mutual trade in manufactures cannot be realised.

A further limitation on the growth of East–West trade is the tight economic interdependence among the E.E. countries. The long-term commitments in production specialisation within COMECON pre-empts trading opportunities with the West in both directions. As we have seen, 60 per cent of members' total trade is with each other. This heavy reliance on intra-bloc trade also tends to perpetuate the notoriously low quality and high prices of most Eastern manufactured goods.

Turning now to trade impediments in the rest of the world, strategic embargoes, export licensing and limitations on export credit and insurance have been important in the past during the period of economic warfare practised against the Eastern bloc by Western Europe, and especially the United States. These restrictions have declined in importance since the late 1950s with the improvement in East—West relations. Today the East European complaints are against Western protectionist policies. In particular they focus their criticism on Western import quotas and other non-tariff barriers, the E.E.C.'s Common Agricultural Policy and the U.S. denial of most-favoured-nation status (MFN) to some E.E. countries (currently only Poland and Romania enjoy MFN treatment by the United States). The Soviet Union, in particular, regards MFN status as a symbol of normalised relations similar to diplomatic recognition; and this has been accepted by the United States. Poland, Romania and recently Hungary have joined the General Agreement on Tariffs and Trade (GATT). In joining GATT these countries have received assurances that GATT members (including the United States) would gradually phase out their discriminatory restrictions in return for assurances from the acceding nations themselves as to improved Western access to Eastern markets. In regard to the E.E.C. the Common Agricultural Policy (CAP) has limited Eastern, in particular Polish, agricultural exports to the E.E.C. Hungary has also suffered from E.E.C. restrictions. The E.E.C. embargo on the import of beef cattle in 1974 (due to overproduction in the Community) cost Hungary the equivalent of $100m. In addition, as a consequence of the Common Market's import prohibition, the export price of Hungarian beef cattle fell by 20 per cent.[6] But the stumbling block here has been the steadfast refusal of the COMECON countries, led by the Soviet Union, to recognise the reality of the E.E.C. However, with the enlargement of the Community and the implementation in January 1975 of the E.E.C's Common Commercial Policy, the E.E. countries have changed their attitude. Several of these countries have worked out special trade agreements with the E.E.C. Commission. As a member of GATT Poland has recently concluded an agreement with the E.E.C. on a new textile export agreement. Ultimately these moves could lead to bloc-to-bloc trade negotiations between the E.E.C. and COMECON, although COMECON is not yet an organisation that has the power to negotiate for its members. Faced with large balance of payments deficits with the E.E.C. and growing debt repayments COMECON leaders have every incentive to seek an accommodation with the Common Market. The February 1977 fishing agreement with the Soviet Union was significant in that the Russians for the first time gave *de facto* recognition to the Common Market. The Russians came to Brussels to negotiate a long-term framework agreement on fisheries following the Community's declaration of its 200-mile fishing zone. E.E. countries now have a wider access to Western credit sources. Apart from loans from Western governments and commercial banks they can secure funds from their own banking institutions which have been set up to tap Western financial markets and to finance East–West trade. Most E.E. countries have also borrowed large amounts directly on Western capital markets, e.g. the Eurocurrency market through syndicated bank loans and credits.

Now we have looked at the barriers, some minor, others more intractable, to the expansion of East–West trade, it is time to assess the current situation and discuss the prospects.

3.3 Prospects

What are the prospects for expanded East–West trade? The most promising trend is the increasing interest of Western firms in doing business with the Eastern bloc countries. These firms are finding that a new type of entrepreneurship is enabling them to overcome many of the traditional obstacles. Eager for Western technology, equipment and credits, E.E. countries are responding to the initiatives of Western businessmen in a manner quite unthinkable only a few years ago. There are now various forms of economic, commercial and technical collaboration between Western firms and Eastern enterprises. Perhaps the most common is the co-production operation under which each side supplies components for the finished product, with the Western firm often undertaking to market the product. Typically, the Western firm supplies the technologically more advanced items and the Eastern enterprise specialises in the more labour-intensive product. Technical assistance, training of personnel and possibly a licence may also be included in such co-production agreements. Another form of East—West business co-operation is the project agreement. Under these agreements Western firms provide the plant designs and technology and supply most of the sophisticated equipment. The Eastern enterprises take much of the responsibility for construction and supply the simpler equipment. An outstandingly successful example of such East—West industrial co-operation is the recently completed Kama Truck Works at Naberezhniye Chelny on the Kama river, some 500 miles east of Moscow. The main contractors for this project, reckoned to be the largest truck factory in the world, were Renault (France), Swindell-Dressler (United States) and Liebherr Gear Works (West Germany). Over one hundred other Western firms participated in the project and supplied equipment or technology under licence to a total value of $1000m.[7] U.S. firms now participate in Soviet resource development, e.g. natural gas, through so-called 'compensation arrangements'. These schemes call for U.S. capital, equipment and know-how on credit, with U.S. firms taking payment in product flows until the initial outlay is paid off. Besides selling resources, Soviet officials expect that in time their industry can become competitive in selling manufactured goods in the United States.

New frontiers in East—West trade are being opened up with the establishment of direct equity participation of Western firms in Eastern enterprises, involving profit-sharing and management participation. This has been possible in Yugoslavia since 1967, and is now being contemplated or tried out in Hungary, Romania and Poland. Such joint venture arrangements offer E.E. countries opportunities to import technological and managerial know-how and to gain access to convertible currency markets. Volvo and Siemens are two well-known Western firms that have set up industrial joint ventures in Hungary. In the majority of co-production deals Western firms have not received payment in money, but rather in kind, in the form of part of the output. These transactions, outside the monetary sphere, are particularly attractive to the East Europeans in view of the inconvertibility of their currencies and their precarious balance of payments positions. One result of the elaboration of co-operative agreements is that they are slowly bringing the multinational corporation to the Eastern European scene. Multinational corporations may have a special advantage in doing business with the East arising out of the peculiar bilateral constraint in East—West trade. With their worldwide sourcing and distribution networks multinational firms can readily accommodate themselves to the exigencies of bilateral trade. For instance, when selling to an E.E. country, a multinational firm can arrange to supply products from a particular Western country with which the Eastern trade partner has a bilateral trade surplus; or, when forced to accept Eastern goods in part payment for exports, these firms can easily dispose of the goods through their regular distribution channels.

Co-operative deals, agreements on the sharing of science and technology and joint enterprises are all aspects of a growing awareness of East—West economic interdependence. To the extent that such deals and exchanges are based on comparative advantage the gains from the trade thereby generated are mutually beneficial. Despite the irrationality of Soviet micro planning it appears that Soviet trade, both in aggregate and in particular markets, conforms to the predictions of the Heckscher—Ohlin theory of comparative advantage.[8] We have no firm evidence for a similar rational basis in respect of the foreign trade of the smaller E.E. countries, but the character of the various co-operative deals with Western enterprises seems to indicate E.E. concern with efficient factor use based on relative factor endowments.[9] Given that future East—West trade will be determined by the prospect of pecuniary advantage from individual transactions, further expansion of trade will depend on (*a*) increases in demand in both sets of markets and (*b*) a further net reduction of impediments. Demand for imports in Eastern Europe will certainly increase, but the limitations in satisfying that demand will be E.E. ability to earn foreign exchange. In the short run tourism provides a valuable source of foreign exchange for countries like Hungary, Bulgaria and Romania. Estimates indicate that, in 1971, Western tourist revenue accounted for 13.5 per cent of E.E. exports to the West. Tourist revenues in these countries grew more rapidly than their visible exports during the 1960s.[10] This expansionary trend is likely to continue. Nevertheless, despite some scope for increasing E.E. import capacity from this source, export performance will be crucial in the long run.

And so we return to the basic institutional factors impeding Eastern penetration of Western markets. One hope is that domestic economic reforms in these countries will hasten the improvement of manufacturing technology and exporting techniques. Acceptance of the conditions required in industrial co-operation with Western market economies will also tend to push E.E. economies further in the direction of economic change needed to improve export performance. However, the E.E. countries are in the process of a wide-ranging programme of economic integration (the 'Complex Programme' adopted at a COMECON meeting in Bucharest, July 1971) involving the co-ordination of long-term national plans and specialisation in production.[11] The Soviet Union is seeking to foster increased integration particularly in the fuel and power industries of COMECON (mainly in Soviet territory) by means of joint investment projects. COMECON members have agreed to share the cost of developing the Orenburg gas deposit in the Soviet Union, including the building of a 2750-km pipeline to get the gas to the Soviet Union's western border. Other co-operative schemes to exploit Soviet natural resources are planned. The Soviet Union has been calling for such co-operation from its neighbours since the late 1960s; it took the 1973 oil crisis and the escalation of commodity prices to spur the E.E. partners into action. Western observers are sceptical that COMECON integration and production specialisation will do much to improve manufacturing export capacity of the smaller E.E. countries. They also fear that tighter integration would slow up market-type reforms by involving greater centralisation of decision-making, which would inevitably imply integration of the smaller economies with the Soviet national economy. But COMECON integration efforts have not been outstandingly successful in the past, and it remains to be seen whether the chances are any better this time. Already they have had to put back to 1990 (from 1980) the goal of full planning integration. The blame for this temporary setback has been placed on Western inflationary trends over the past three years which have resulted in sharp increases in imported prices of oil, commodities and capital equipment.[12]

COMECON planners were forced to keep pace with the rises in world market prices. Prices of fuel and raw materials were raised in inter-COMECON trade from the beginning of 1975. Although the price of Russian oil delivered to its COMECON partners rose substantially (by 130 per cent) it was still about a third cheaper than OPEC prices. However, the price of Russian oil has been rising steadily on the basis of the sliding-scale formula agreed within COMECON in 1975. By 1978 the price of Soviet oil deliveries is likely to approach the world level. COMECON co-operation is seen by many E.E. leaders as the only viable option for coping with a particularly difficult economic situation. Western inflation, including in particular escalating energy prices, the global shortage of raw materials and Western recession have saddled the E.E. countries with enormous trade deficits and external debt. In this parlous situation the E.E. countries have no choice but to rely on the Soviet Union for essential supplies of fuel and raw materials to keep industrial production at current levels – let alone to continue the modernisation and expansion of existing facilities. They cannot afford to allocate scarce convertible currency for fuel and raw materials purchases in the West or Third World countries. Hence, the growing number of joint investment projects to develop energy supplies in Soviet territory.[13] The fact is, however, that integration in Eastern Europe is hampered by the differences in price and wage systems and by the non-existence of convertible national currencies. Nevertheless, despite the forces in COMECON tending towards increased emphasis on self-reliance, the commercial links forged between East and West could easily ensure that mutual trade expands in the years ahead at a rate no less than the 11 per cent annual rate experienced during the past decade. This would certainly be the case if there is a moderation in the rate of global inflation and a speedy economic revival in the West.

Further Reading

R. E. Caves and R. W. Jones, *World Trade and Payments* (Boston, Mass.: Little, Brown & Co. 1973) chap. 15, sec. 4

F. D. Holzman, *International Trade Under Communism: Politics and Economics* (London: Macmillan, 1976). An excellent account of the main influences on East—West trade.

S. Pisar, *Coexistence & Commerce* (London: Allen Lane The Penguin Press, 1970). A discursive treatment of the economic and political background to East—West trade.

J. Wilczynski, *The Economics and Politics of East—West Trade* (London: Macmillan, 1969).

J. Wilczynski, *The Multinationals and East—West Relations* (London: Macmillan, 1976). An expert in the field discusses the role of MNCs (both capitalist and socialist) in East—West business co-operation.

CHAPTER 4

The Eurodollar Market, Short-term Capital Flows and Currency Crises

Central bankers have had an unusually hard time these last five or six years. Added to their problem of having to contend with severe inflation they have had to cope with the disruptive effects of vast flows of short-term capital. These capital flows have undermined the effectiveness of national monetary policies and have precipitated currency crises. The effects have been particularly felt in Europe, but even the United States did not remain unscathed during the international monetary whirlwind of 1971 and 1973. Speculative flights out of U.S. dollars forced two devaluations on the United States during these years, wrecking the Bretton Woods fixed exchange rate system in the process. During these crises of the early 1970s the Eurodollar market was often blamed for contributing to, if not actually being the cause of, this state of affairs. There were frequent calls for international action to control this largely unregulated private market in short-term monetary assets. Now that exchange rates of the principal currencies are floating, and the Eurodollar market is successfully handling the gigantic task of recycling oil receipts, calls for control are muted; but some observers remain suspicious, while others worry about its future stability. What, then, is the Eurodollar market? How does the market generate increased capital mobility? How can the market weaken the effectiveness of national monetary policies? What is its role in currency crises? Is the market to blame for world inflation? What of its future? In this chapter we try to answer these questions. First, we examine the rationale of the Eurodollar market.

4.1 Rationale of the Eurodollar Market[1]

The Eurodollar market is an international credit market operating outside the United States in which banks (Euro-banks) accept dollar deposits from investors and extend dollar loans. Eurodollars can be defined very briefly as deposit liabilities, denominated in dollars, of banks outside the United States; they include deposits in foreign branches of U.S. banks. A bank accepting a Eurodollar deposit receives, in settlement of the transaction, a dollar balance with a bank in the United States. A bank making a Eurodollar deposit or loan completes the transaction with a transfer from its U.S. bank balance. To grasp the essence of Eurodollar operations consider the following, rather typical, example. An American chemical company in Chicago instructs its bank to transfer $2 million from its account to the Eurodollar market in London because Euro-banks there are paying higher interest rates. The transfer leaves the U.S. company with a dollar deposit in a London bank, while the London bank has a dollar deposit in the Chicago bank. The London bank then deposits the funds in a Euro-bank in Milan at the London interbank interest rate. The Milan bank, in turn, extends a $2 million loan to an Italian construction company at a lower rate than the building firm would pay for a lira loan from a domestic bank. The Italian firm now uses the loan to pay for equipment imported from Germany. The Eurodollar market thus serves as a financial intermediary, bringing lenders and borrowers together on an international basis.

Table 4.1 shows the recent growth of the total Eurocurrency market. Various reasons have been given for the existence and rapid development of the market (from a few hundred million dollars in 1957 to $180,000m. in 1976). These include (*a*) the Sterling crisis of 1957 which led to the imposition of tight controls on non-resident borrowing and lending by U.K. banks encouraged London banks to offer the same financing facilities in dollars instead, (*b*) the rigid structure of interest rates in the domestic banking system of the U.S. with (at various periods) its wide margins between borrowing and lending rates, allowing plenty of room for non-U.S. banks to

Table 4.1

Growth of the Eurocurrency Market, 1965–77* Net Size (billions of U.S. dollars)

Year	Net size
1965	10
1966	15
1967	17
1968	24
1969	44
1970	57
1971	70
1972	91
1973	132
1974	177
1975	205
1976	247

Source: BIS, *Annual Reports*.
* This covers only the part of the market which is accounted for by banks or countries reporting to the Bank for International Settlements.

borrow and lend in dollars in large amounts at much finer margins and still take a comfortable profit, (*c*) the advent of convertibility (1958) and the associated relaxation of exchange controls over banking transactions in Europe, (*d*) the switch of dollar balances in the early Cold War days by some E.E. countries from U.S. banks to European banks for fear that their deposits might be blocked or confiscated, (*e*) at least up to 1971 (and again since 1973) some central banks were motivated to place part of their reserves in the market in order to secure the highest return on their dollar assets, (*f*) the large deficit in the U.S. balance of payments after 1957 which, it is claimed, provided a plentiful supply of funds to European banks which they chose to relend abroad rather than convert into local currencies, (*g*) because Euro-banks are not subject to official reserve requirements (which for other domestic banks constitute a 'tax' on their earnings), their costs are low – hence, they can pay more on deposits and charge less for loans than their domestic counterparts. At a more fundamental level the rationale of the Eurodollar market lies in the 'vehicle-currency' use of the dollar. Despite the ravages of inflation and two devaluations the dollar is the vehicle currency in international trade and finance, i.e. apart from its use as a reserve currency, the U.S. dollar is widely used as a medium of exchange, a *numéraire* and method of holding wealth by traders, individuals, oil-rich states and institutions throughout the world. Over one-third of the world trade (currently running at $1000 billions) is financed – and probably even more denominated – in dollars. The dollar has fulfilled the needs of the world business community for a genuinely international currency and international money market. These needs in turn reflect the convenience and economic advantages to be derived from concentrating international commercial and financial transactions in a single currency. This being the case, it is not surprising that foreign markets in the vehicle currency should develop; when sterling was the international vehicle currency before 1914 banks outside the United Kingdom took deposits and granted credits in sterling.

There can be little doubt that the existence of the Eurodollar market has greatly increased the international movement of short-term capital. High capital mobility is a phenomenon peculiarly associated with the Eurodollar market. For investors the major media for international money-market operations are now obligations of commercial banks denominated in currencies other than their own, i.e. Eurodollar deposits are popular, attractive substitutes for other financial assets, and particularly for time deposits in domestic currency and short-term money market instruments such as Treasury bills, certificates of deposit (CDs) and commercial paper. Increased capital mobility can also be traced to the same nexus of external dollar deposits and vehicle-currency use for the simple reason that Eurodollar deposits make better vehicles for capital movements than others. The availability of these international vehicle assets (Eurodollars) facilitates investor responsiveness to international interest-rate differentials by reducing the amount of risk and inconvenience inherent in holding foreign assets – thereby increasing the amount of capital moving abroad in response to given interest-rate differentials. The risks and inconvenience associated with foreign short-term investment stem from the denomination of assets in different currencies (risk of unfavourable exchange-rate changes),[2] the possibility of exchange controls and other national restrictions being imposed and imperfect knowledge of conditions in foreign money markets. The Eurodollar market mitigates these inconveniences in a number of ways.

In the first place it offers a new menu of assets widely available at short term, all denominated in a single vehicle currency. Obviously, for American investors, no exchange-rate risk is incurred by placing funds in the market. As for non-U.S. investors, they have the option of making foreign currency loans to familiar, local institutions such as nationalised industries and local authorities without having to worry about exchange controls or the financial standing of distant borrowers.

Second, the growing international network of banking connections fostered by the Eurodollar market has broken down the barriers to the flow of information on economic and credit conditions in national markets with the result that investors now have reliable and up-to-date intelligence to go on.

Third, since Euro-banks are still less regulated than domestic banks, Eurodollar business often passes through the net of national exchange controls, particularly transactions that take the form of loans to non-banks.

In addition to decreasing the risk and inconvenience involved in foreign money-market operations the Eurodollar market has helped to integrate both the money and foreign exchange markets of the six largest countries on both sides of the Atlantic. This is a further instance of the way in which the Eurodollar market has promoted greater capital mobility. The structure of the market is such that banking operations in the dollar are decentralised down to the particular location of borrowers and lenders in the different financial centres. This permits an intricate pattern of interest arbitraging transactions between individual national money markets and the Euro-dollar market. Because Euro-banks are willing to arbitrage in this way the interest rates on comparable securities differ only by the spread between the forward and spot exchange rates. Small interest-rate discrepancies outside these limits are enough to set in motion vast capital flows. By interposing itself in the midst of the national money markets, linking them together, the Eurodollar market brings about a situation where European and American investors now perceive foreign and domestic assets as close substitutes. A recent study found evidence of close substitutability between covered 3-month Eurodollar deposits and 3-month deutschmark money market loans.[3]

High substitutability between foreign and domestic securities is, of course, an essential attribute of a state of perfect capital mobility. By reducing risk and integrating financial markets the Eurodollar market tends to increase the interest-elasticity of international short-term capital, i.e. it reduces the slope of both the supply and demand curves for external funds in the world money market. What we have emerging is a picture of a unified international money market with funds flowing freely from one centre to another according to variations in interest rates and the possibilities of exchange risks.

Now this environment of high capital mobility generated by the Eurodollar market is bound to impede the pursuit of an independent monetary policy by any small or medium-sized country trying to stabilise prices and employment within its borders. How constraining is this influence of the market, and how have European central bankers coped with it? To suggest answers to these questions we turn to the impact of the Eurodollar market on the effectiveness of monetary policy in Europe during the 1960s and early 1970s – a period during which, in the environment we have been describing, individual European countries were attempting to use monetary policy for domestic purposes under conditions of external surpluses and fixed exchange rates.

4.2 The Eurodollar Market and Monetary Policy in Europe

The restoration of convertibility after 1958, the gradual dismantling of exchange restrictions and the re-emergence of international banking were the first signals for the revival of capital mobility among European countries. Interest arbitrage operations again assumed their traditional role; speculative and precautionary flows (including 'leads and lags') were also inevitable in the climate of greater freedom. But, as was mentioned earlier, the emergence of the Eurodollar market greatly added to these traditional inter-country flows of capital and greatly complicated the problems faced by European monetary authorities. The potential impact of the market assumed threatening proportions as early as 1965 when total Eurodollar claims of over $21 million exceeded the money supply in a few countries.

The early Eurodollar-oriented flows stemmed from the monopolistic practices maintained by several European commercial banks, competitive facilities offered by the Eurodollar market and the growing rigidity of exchange rates after 1958. Because of the high interest rates on commercial loans in many European countries and the fact that rates were generally lower in the Eurodollar market, exporters and importers switched from domestic to foreign currency credits for ordinary trade financing; later they borrowed foreign currency for domestic requirements. As changes in exchange parities became less and less likely, European banks, responding to the demand, began using Eurodollars for domestic lending purposes. They converted dollars in the spot market against their national currencies and purchased the dollars back in the forward market; but in some cases they maintained uncovered positions in order to save the cost of forward cover. This was especially true in Italy and Germany. In Italy, at the inception of the Eurodollar market, rate structures for domestic loans were high and rigid. Commercial banks had for a long time followed a practice, based on tacit agreement, of not lending money to their customers at rates below 6 per cent plus commissions and taxes. Up to the end of 1960 foreign currency facilities were not subject to these rate agreements. Consequently, Italian importers found it advantageous to have their purchases from abroad financed by their bankers in Eurocurrencies, primarily Eurodollars. At first the bankers charged rates somewhat lower than the going rate of 6 per cent for domestic loans; however, when competition among the banks intensified, rates were reduced to as low as $3\frac{1}{2}$ per cent.

In Germany the situation was similar and developments followed the same course. Short-term interest rates were high, and even the largest companies could not get overdraft accommodation in DM. for less than the minimum rates of 6–$6\frac{1}{2}$ per cent. This rate structure made the Eurodollar market quite attractive for domestic working capital purposes. Companies began borrowing more and more in the Eurodollar market and converting the funds into DM. with or without covering their positions. Thus the market became of considerable importance to the German monetary authorities; for here was a novel challenge to the traditional instruments of monetary control.

Now, there is a vast theoretical literature[4] (pioneered by Robert Mundell) which shows in the hypothetical limit, that if all money markets are fully integrated and capital perfectly mobile in a world of fixed exchange rates it would be impossible for any small country alone to use monetary policy in pursuit of domestic objectives. In fact it could control neither its money supply nor its level of interest rates. If the monetary authorities, for example, attempt to curtail domestic demand by raising interest rates they would simply invite an inflow of capital from abroad (in this context, from the Eurodollar market), thus vitiating the restrictive policy. Similarly, an attempt at monetary ease would stimulate a capital outflow, not domestic demand. The moral is clear – in a regime of fixed exchange rates and perfect capital mobility a small country must assign monetary policy to the goal of maintaining balance of payments equilibrium, while fiscal policy must carry the burden of domestic income stabilisation. Monetary policy cannot, therefore, be used in pursuit of full employment, price stability or economic growth. On the other hand, monetary policy becomes effective for these purposes when exchange rates are flexible; flexible exchange rates break the link between international capital flows and changes in domestic cash reserves.

It is not the purpose of this section to go into the ramifications of the theoretical model which produces this result; however, the reasoning is basically simple and can be put as follows: In a closed economy $S-I=G-T$ describes equilibrium in the market for goods and services, where $S-I$ is the excess of saving over intended investment, i.e. excess demand for new securities in the private sector, and $G-T$ is the budget deficit, i.e. excess supply of new government securities.

Because an excess demand for new securities would tend to depress the equilibrium level of income, this tendency would be counteracted to the extent that the government runs a budget deficit equal to the excess demand for securities generated in the private sector.

The situation is similar in an open economy with perfect capital mobility, i.e. macroeconomic equilibrium is perfectly compatible with a deficit or surplus in the trade balance as long as capital mobility permits such deficits and surpluses to be financed by offsetting capital flows. That is to say, abstracting from government, in a two-country world, equilibrium requires:

$$I_1 - S_1 \; = \; M_1 - X_1 \; = \; S_2 - I_2,$$

i.e. the excess supply of new securities in country 1 must equal the excess demand for new securities in country 2; and each country's excess supply of new securities equals its trade deficit, to preserve balance of payments equilibrium. This is the basic mechanism that ensures simultaneous equilibrium in the two countries. Now, to see the limitation of monetary policy as an instrument of domestic stabilisation, assume an increase in the money supply, i.e. by open-market purchases of securities in the domestic economy designed to increase the level of income. The open-market operation has the effect of reducing domestic interest rates and therefore leads to a capital outflow. The monetary authority must now sell foreign exchange to prevent its price from rising, and in so doing contracts the domestic money supply. Equilibrium cannot be re-established until the interest-rate differential is eliminated. Thus the level of income fails to rise by this route, and the only effect of the open-market operation is to replace a portion of the foreign exchange assets of the monetary authority with domestic assets – the capital export exactly cancels the increase in the domestically-created credit base. We conclude, therefore, that monetary policy under fixed exchange rates and capital mobility is a means of controlling the level of foreign exchange reserves, but is essentially powerless to affect the domestic money supply and, therefore, the level of economic activity.

Fiscal policy would suffer no such disability as a domestic

stabiliser. Under these circumstances monetary policy can be used to influence the balance of payments; a country could 'finance' a deficit by tightening credit at home in order to induce an inflow of funds from abroad, i.e. the Eurodollar market. The popular appeal of Mundell's simple model at the time it was presented (the early 1960s when fixed exchange rates were the rule) lay in the fact that it suggested an optimum policy-mix formula whereby a country could attain full employment and equilibrium in the balance of payments by the proper assignment of monetary and fiscal policy instruments to the two policy targets. It appeared to offer a useful rule-of-thumb for situations where the authorities had limited knowledge of the economic system. It prescribed a set of policy responses that converged on equilibrium, so that the authorities had merely to know the current state of the balance of payments and the level of unemployment and adjust interest rates and the budget deficit accordingly to achieve the desired target values for the two objectives. The policy-mix prescription was particularly relevant to the work of IMF officials, who were often called upon to design external adjustment policies for countries where data were inadequate and macroeconomic relationships largely unknown. However, critics of the theory of the policy mix pointed to the limitations and ambiguities surrounding this approach to economic policy in an open economy. It was argued that (1) international capital flows depend on income (which determines the profitability of direct investment) as well as the level of interest rates, so that it is not clear that monetary policy has a comparative advantage in dealing with the balance of payments under fixed exchange rates; (2) the policy mix is not a true adjustment device for external disequilibrium. It merely *finances* a deficit on the current account with an induced capital inflow on the private capital account; (3) welfare costs are incurred in financing balance-of-payments deficits in the way suggested by the theory (the debt-servicing problem) for countries with chronic or structural problems of adjustment. These welfare costs are ignored, no doubt because the model is analogous to an engineering control system, and therefore devoid of normative implications in the economic sense, i.e. no community welfare function is consciously being maximised; (4) the policy mix presupposes that countries have the use of flexible fiscal policy instruments that can be adjusted at short notice to cope with sudden and unexpected changes in internal macroeconomic variables, e.g. the rate of unemployment or the rate of price inflation; (5) finally, of course (as we have indicated), in the limiting case of an infinite interest elasticity of international capital movements (perfect capital mobility) it makes no sense to talk of monetary policy (either in the sense of interest-rate policy or money-supply policy) as being an available instrument of economic policy for most countries. A non-reserve currency country, i.e. a country other than the United States, cannot maintain an interest-rate differential against the world level; neither can it effectively control the domestic money supply under fixed exchange rates. The only meaningful definition of monetary policy for such a country is a change in the portfolio of the central bank through open-market operations. The money supply itself is, via the balance of payments (reserve flows) endogenously determined. Although the achievement of external and internal balance under the old regime of fixed exchange rates proved elusive in practice, Mundell's theoretical analyses and observations on what he called the 'disequilibrium system' led some influential economists to retrace their steps back to the earlier doctrine of David Hume and other classical economists on the role of money in an open economy. The revival of this teaching under the contemporary label of the 'monetary approach to balance-of-payments theory' reinforces the belief that, in an interdependent world, monetary autonomy is largely an illusion.[5]

The interesting question to investigate now is how exactly did European monetary authorities cope with such an environment. Their problems were further complicated by the fact that the beginning of increased capital mobility coincided with a period of massive external surpluses. Here one had the makings of the classic textbook dilemma in the form of a stark conflict between the requirements for domestic balance and external balance: to avoid the inflationary implications of a trade surplus a tight monetary policy was called for; but a tight monetary policy would attract additional foreign capital perhaps at an accelerating pace, thereby exacerbating the difficulties of 'neutralising' the domestic impact of the payments surplus. Even if there were no interest-sensitive capital movements, payments surpluses on the scale experienced by some European countries in this early period were bound seriously to threaten central banks' control over the credit base. The non-viability of sterilisation operations soon became manifest – especially (if for no other reason) in view of the limited capacities of European financial markets to absorb offsetting operations by their central banks. Traditional techniques such as discount policy and reserve requirements were regarded by many as inadequate tools in this new environment. Professor Friedrich Lutz, for example, referring pointedly to the German experience in this type of situation declared quite categorically: 'The Central Bank is bound to lose control of the money supply, and therefore over the level of total spending.'[6] With increased mobility of capital supervening in this already critical situation the problem posed, quite frankly, was how to devise *effective* ways of sterilising the excess domestic liquidity created by the payments surpluses without at the same time provoking unwanted inflows of private capital.

Quite naturally, in the circumstances, they turned to administrative controls in order to stem the tide, e.g. prohibition of interest payments to foreigners, special reserve requirements on foreigners' deposits, etc. But a more positive approach was to use a technique that might be called 'open-market operations in the Eurodollar market'. Because of the flexibility of the commercial banks' foreign positions, measures to induce banks to make marginal liquidity adjustments in their foreign (Eurodollar) rather than in their domestic positions became the principal regulatory device. Not only could this device be used to regain control over domestic liquidity, but equally it was efficacious on the external balance side, since its use determines the net flow of private short-term capital and hence the amount of financing that has to be done through official reserves.

The procedure is simple. By means of forward 'swap' transactions the central bank offers commercial banks attractive rates on forward sales of dollars, thus increasing the covered yield to the banks on investments denominated in dollars; the banks are thus induced to hold assets abroad in foreign currency, thereby absorbing excess domestic liquidity and increasing the cost of borrowing in domestic currency. One can alternatively describe the procedure as a substitution of forward exchange policy for monetary policy.

This technique, supplemented by *ad hoc* exchange controls, enabled monetary authorities to cope fairly satisfactorily with the Eurodollar market; but these mechanisms broke down in the late 1960s and early 1970s in the face of unprecedented currency upheavals. As a result of the crises, however, the lesson has been learnt (if not rigorously followed in practice) that monetary independence today is a fragile creature when countries attempt to fix the exchange value of their currencies. While it is recognised that a floating exchange rate strengthens monetary policy when domestic goals are at stake (such as the money supply or demand management) countries are still reluctant to gain the full benefits of this extra degree of monetary freedom for fear of causing sudden changes in the international competitive positions of businesses in their countries – the risk implicit in free floating.

So, in the meantime, exchange rates are being 'managed', either by governments trying to maintain a single preferred rate with a greater flexibility than in the past, or by operating two-tier exchange-rate systems. The latter system is one in which capital transactions are required to pass through a financial exchange market where exchange rates are floating, while trade transactions pass through an official market where rates are pegged within narrow limits by the monetary authority. Belgium has used a dual exchange rate system for over fifteen years, and both France (1971) and Italy (1973) introduced the system in an effort to control capital flows during the recent currency crises. The next section continues the discussion of the role of capital flows – this time in the context of currency crises.

4.3 Currency Crises

The last ten years have witnessed periods of unsettled conditions in foreign exchange markets stemming from currency uncertainties provoking massive speculative flows of funds. In such conditions the movement of internationally-owned private funds can reach amounts of the order of thousands of millions of dollars in a matter of days, as during the period 3–5

May 1971 prior to the floating of the German mark ($2000m.), or in mid-August the same year when $4000m. flowed into foreign official reserves as firms and individuals took steps to protect their assets from the expected depreciation of the dollar against other currencies.

Now the significance of the Eurodollar market is that it facilitates the movement of such flights of capital from one currency to another. Besides being an attractive entrepôt for trading and investment funds, at times of currency uncertainty the market becomes swollen with 'hot' money ready to rebound with anonymity in any direction, to any country, into any currency. Currency uncertainty such as we have experienced in recent years gives rise to a demand for Eurodollars for switching into gold (1967–8), Deutschmarks (1969 and 1971) or other European currencies and the Yen (1971). Massive movements of funds motivated by the search for protection against possible currency devaluations or by the search for speculative gains from revaluations may be magnified by the Eurodollar market's intermediation; but the market is the scene, not the cause.

Basically, currency crises such as we have had until 1973 reflect two underlying factors. First, the desire of countries to pursue independent monetary policies in an integrated world economy, and, second, the commitment of the major trading countries to fixed exchange rates. Now, of course, as we have discussed previously, monetary independence is incompatible with fixed exchange rates. Countries at different phases of the business cycle will have divergent trends in their monetary conditions and policies. Price and wage levels would rise rapidly in some countries and slowly in others. For the country that prefers a lower rate of inflation than the world average for domestic purposes the result will be an increased foreign demand for exports and a switch of demand from imports to domestic substitutes. This implies a balance of payments surplus, an increase in official reserves as the central bank sells domestic currency to maintain the fixed rate and an expansion of the monetary base. The attempt to reduce domestic liquidity is likely to induce an inflow of short-term capital and aggravate the situation. A revaluation of the currency may ultimately be necessary. In general, these divergencies in price levels lead to balance of payments disequilibria with some currencies under-valued and others overvalued, i.e. some currencies become 'strong' while others appear 'weak'. When that happens, speculators move against the weak currencies by selling them in the market and purchasing the currencies perceived to be strong; under a pegged exchange rate system they can hardly lose (speculators have a riskless one-way option) and may realise a considerable profit by acting together on the basis of market signals. Estimates indicate that during the crisis years 1967–71 speculators made net profits of $5000m. largely at the expense of central banks trying to defend unrealistic parities. It is the persistence of unrealistic currency values that gives rise to speculative activity in foreign exchange markets.

The basic problem in the 1971 and 1973 currency crises was that the international monetary system could not promote effective balance of payments adjustment, given the conflicting policy objectives of fixed parity rates and the pursuit of independent monetary policies. The conflict became more intense as the integration of economies and capital markets continued. Chronic payments surpluses and deficits main-tained a gap between the official international values of currencies and their domestic values. The increased awareness that prevailing exchange rates were inappropriate generated the large-scale speculative capital flows that eventually forced the authorities in leading industrial countries to adopt some form of flexible exchange rate, i.e. 'managed' floating.

Between 1967 and early 1971 there were at least six exchange crises involving in each case a particular currency, such as the pound sterling (1967), the French franc (1968), the German mark (September 1969 and May 1971), the Swiss franc (May 1971) and the Austrian schilling (May 1971). There was no systematic relation between the problems of sterling, the French franc and the Swiss franc. The problem of each currency stemmed from the continued maintenance of unre-alistic exchange rates. But the dollar crisis in the summer of 1971 was of a different order; it involved more than ten countries. The primary cause of this crisis was the persistent deficit in the U.S. balance of payments leading to a lack of confidence in the dollar, and a speculative flight from this into other currencies, notably the German mark.

The Eurodollar market did not play a particularly destabilising role in the crisis. There was little evidence of a run on the dollar through withdrawals of deposits from the market, as might have been feared. What happened was that in 1970 and 1971 monetary policies in the United States and Europe moved in opposite directions. There was a sharp acceleration in credit expansion in the United States at a time when, owing to rising inflationary pressures in Europe, European countries were turning towards increasingly restrictive monetary policies. As a result of easier credit conditions in the United States, American banks repaid over $6000m. to their overseas branches in the Eurodollar market. The bulk of these funds was absorbed on an unprecedented scale by foreign bank and non-bank borrowers for conversion into foreign currencies. In addition to outright speculation facilitated by the Eurodollar market much of the pressure on the dollar reflected 'leads and lags' and hedging in commercial transactions as U.S. firms with payments due in foreign currencies accelerated those payments, while foreign businessmen delayed dollar payments in anticipation of a dollar depreciation *vis-à-vis* other currencies. Foreign exporters who anticipated dollar receipts borrowed spot dollars in the Eurodollar market, then switched into strong currencies, e.g. the Deutschmark, by placing the funds temporarily in Germany or the Euro-DM. market. When subsequently received the dollar proceeds were used to liquidate the Eurodollar credit. At the same time U.S. firms transferred large amounts of funds to their European affiliates and subsidiaries. To the extent that 'leads and lags' and hedging were significant sources of strain such strains would have been manifested anyway even if the Eurodollar market had not existed.

As evidence continued to accumulate that the underlying deficit in the U.S. external accounts was large and increasing (a development that made clear the extent to which the dollar had become overvalued and convinced the markets that the dollar's turn to be devalued had finally arrived) the rush out of dollars accelerated. The demand for other currencies increased in intensity, with one foreign currency after another the focus of speculative forays as a general run on the dollar developed. As these short-term funds moved across the exchanges European and Japanese monetary authorities had to absorb dollars from the market in order to prevent the appreciation of their currencies against the dollar, thereby swelling the money stocks of these countries. By 15 August 1971, when the United States announced the suspension of dollar covertibility, liquid dollar liabilities to foreign official institutions were more than three times larger than the United States reserve holdings.

The currency upheaval subsided with the U.S. suspension of gold sales and the floating of major currencies. The general realignment of exchange rates, including the devaluation of the dollar in December 1971 further calmed exchange markets. But only fourteen months later this comparative tranquillity was shattered as another round of speculation swept away the last vestiges of the fixed-exchange-rate system. This time, however, the strain on the international economy was greatly magnified by the quadrupling of the price of crude oil and the consequent large and rapid deterioration in the trade balances of the oil-consuming countries in favour of the oil exporters. In the long run the oil price rise poses a classical 'transfer problem', in that a real transfer of wealth must be made from the oil-importing countries either through trade or capital transactions. The short-run financial problem is one of 'recycling' the massive payments surpluses of the oil-producing countries back to the consuming countries. The Eurodollar market, being one of the main channels for international capital flows, has found itself with the task of intermediating the oil funds between the deficit and surplus countries. Eurocurrency placements by OPEC members were estimated at about one-third of these countries' aggregate investible surpluses – the amount of the oil surplus left over after expenditures for imports and loans and grants to less developed countries – in 1974. Table 4.2 estimates how OPEC has been disposing of its total investible surplus. These funds have been borrowed by the oil-importing countries to help finance their deficits. In this intermediary role the Eurodollar market faces a severe test; but so far, at any rate, the market has performed creditably. The market has exercised a stabilising influence, as it makes it easier for countries to finance their oil deficits and thus tends to calm down exchange markets. Initially, however, there were some fears that as the recycling process got into its stride Euro-banks might face

Table 4.2

Estimated Disposition of OPEC Surpluses (in billions of U.S. dollars)

	1974	1975	1976
Bank deposits and money-market placements:			
Dollar deposits in United States	4.0	0.6	1.6
Sterling deposits in United Kingdom	1.7	0.2	−1.4
Eurocurrency deposits	22.8	9.1	12.6
Treasury bills in United States and United Kingdom	8.0	−0.4	−2.2
Long-term investments:			
Special bilateral arrangements	11.9	12.4	10.3
International Institutions	3.5	4.0	2.0
Govt securities in United States and United Kingdom	1.1	2.4	4.4
Other	4.0	7.4	8.0
Total new investments	57.0	35.7	35.3

Source: BIS, *Annual Report*, June 1977, p. 92.

liquidity problems. And, indeed, in 1974 the combination of erratic exchange rates, huge payments deficits, world-wide inflation and a rapid growth in banks' balance sheets produced some pressures on the international banking community. The ratio of Euro-banks' short-term liabilities to capital rose towards the limits set by prudent management. Difficulties were experienced in intermediating loans to countries with large external debts as banks sought to reduce the risks of loan exposure. Foreign exchange losses were incurred by a few banks as a result of the unfamiliar wider exchange-rate swings. Confidence was restored in 1975 as central bankers reaffirmed their responsibility for the international banking market and agreed to support banks in trouble. Other factors that contributed to the restoration of confidence in the Eurocurrency market included the manifest ability of the private banking system to handle the so-called petrodollar flows, and a better understanding of the dimensions of the oil surplus problem, which now appears more manageable than previously predicted.

Is the rapid growth of the Eurocurrency market to blame for the recent surge of world inflation? We conclude this chapter with a short answer to this question. Some people harbour the suspicion that the Eurocurrency market is behind the pace of global inflation because of the system's potential for expanding world money supply.[7] It is now well established that prices, on the average, respond with a lag of between one to two years to changes in monetary growth in most economies. Since Euro-deposits are held primarily in the form of time deposits they must be considered as money under the broad definition (M_2) used by analysts. Eurocurrency deposits have increased ten times (gross) between 1969 and 1975. Hence, it is argued, the market's expansion must have contributed significantly to the world-wide rate of inflation. However, it is not at all clear that the Eurocurrency system operates in the same manner as a domestic banking system, being capable of a multiple expansion of deposits from an initial quantity of primary deposits or reserves. The analogy with a domestic banking system breaks down because (*a*) in the Euromarket we cannot assume that customers keep a fixed proportion of their assets in the form of Eurodeposits; and (*b*) unlike a domestic banking system, Eurobanks cannot increase their loans and deposits without affecting at the same time relative interest rates. Each trans-action produces a change in relative interest rates and a new demand – supply relationship. Therefore, the idea of a simple fixed-coefficient form for the money multiplier is not appli-cable in the case of the Euromarket. Moreover, positive asset transformation (whereby a domestic banking system lends at relatively long term on the basis of demand deposits) is not characteristic of the Euromarket. A recent empirical study[8] which incorporates these factors in an attempt to estimate the Eurocurrency multiplier found that it was around unity during the period 1968–72. The maximum possible size of the multiplier, including the expansionary impact of central banks deposits, was only 1.4. The authors suggest that the Euro-bank system is nothing more than a network (but an efficient one at that) for the distribution of liquid dollar funds from areas of surplus to areas of deficit in the world economy. They concluded that the impact of the Eurocurrency market on the world money supply has not been very significant. This finding was corroborated by a First National City Bank of New York analysis[9] in 1976, which compared the growth of Eurocurrency deposits from 1965 to 1974 with the growth of the money stock (M_2) of ten leading industrial countries for the corresponding period. FNCY found that over the ten-year period the growth of Eurocurrency deposits added on average less than 1 per cent to the industrial countries' monetary growth. In the light of this evidence it is difficult to maintain that the expansion of the Eurocurrency market has been responsible for the high rate of inflation experienced in recent years. The Euromarket simply distributes around the globe whatever monetary expansion national monetary authorities, individually or collectively, allow. As international financial intermediaries, Eurobanks do serve to increase the velocity of nationally-created money, but this is quite different from having the ability to create money.

Further Reading

G. Bell, *The Eurodollar Market and the International Financial System* (London: Macmillan, 1973).

E. W. Clendenning, *The Euro-Dollar Market* (London: Oxford University Press, 1970).

J. Hewson and E. Sakakibara, *The Euro-currency Markets and their Implications* (Lexington, Mass.: Lexington Books, 1975).

G. W. McKenzie, *The Economics of the Eurocurrency System* (London: Macmillan, 1976).

J. S. Little, *Euro-dollars: The Money Market Gypsies* (New York: Harper & Row, 1975).

CHAPTER 5

World Monetary Arrangements

5.1 The Bretton Woods System

On 15 August 1971 the international monetary arrangements that prevailed since the end of the Second World War ceased to function. On that day the golden anchor was cut loose from the system by the United States announcement that it was no longer prepared to buy and sell gold freely in transactions with foreign monetary authorities. This was the final death blow to the tottering Bretton Woods system, for that system rested formally on the free convertibility of gold by at least one key-currency country, i.e. the United States. Severing the link between the dollar and gold at least temporarily converted the system into a combination of an inconvertible dollar standard and managed floating exchange rates. In effect the world now finds itself in a monetary interregnum pending new arrangements to replace the Bretton Woods system. The old system suffered from serious weaknesses that became increasingly evident from the 1960s onwards (e.g. the succession of currency crises) and there was no shortage of plans, schemes, etc., for reforming the system. In the event the sudden breakdown of the system, although expected for some time, presented the world's financial authorities with the task of devising a new system on the basis of extant plans that hopefully would last another twenty-five years as the Bretton Woods system did.

In this chapter it is appropriate that we begin by examining the design of the Bretton Woods system to see what went wrong and why. Next we analyse the causes and events of the 1971 crisis that finally brought the system down. In the last section we examine some perspectives on the reform of the world's monetary arrangements.

Former U.S. President Nixon referred to the December 1971 Smithsonian Institution agreement on the realignment of exchange rates after the dollar crisis as 'the greatest monetary agreement in history'. But the agreement lasted only fourteen months. With greater justification this title might be claimed for the monetary arrangements set up at Bretton Woods, New Hampshire, in the summer of 1944. Certainly the 1000 delegates from forty-four countries who attended this U.N. Monetary and Financial Conference felt they were engaged in a momentous undertaking. The job to be done was to devise an international monetary system that would rid the new post-war business and financial world community of the chronic monetary instability, currency disorders, excessive trade barriers, exchange restrictions, barter deals and widespread 'beggar-thy-neighbour' policies that paralysed the inter-war world economy. The inter-war period demonstrated the need for an institutional framework that would enable individual countries to follow policies directed towards domestic objectives of full employment and rising living standards without creating problems for others. The delegates had learnt the lessons of the depression years and saw quite clearly that the purpose of international monetary arrangements was to facilitate multilateral trade and investment, and not vice versa. The gold exchange standard had collapsed in the 1930s because it failed to provide a stable monetary environment for conducting free international trade and payments. It allowed the forces of economic nationalism to dictate the conduct of international economic transactions. The spirit of international co-operation was lacking, and this is what the delegates sought to remedy by incorporating in the Articles of Agreement of the institution they set up, i.e. the International Monetary Fund (IMF), rules regulating international financial behaviour. For the first time a monetary system was set up by international agreement, for under the old Gold Standard there was no formal international agreement – only conventions of international monetary policy referred to as 'rules of the game'.

The system set up at Bretton Woods rested on two pillars: the maintenance of stable exchange rates and a multilateral credit mechanism, institutionalised in the IMF and supervised by it. Each member of the IMF undertook to fix an official par value for its currency in terms of gold or the gold equivalent in U.S. dollars and to keep the exchange rate within 1 per cent of the par value by offsetting private excess supplies or demand for its currency in the market by purchases or sales of its currency. Most countries chose to observe the obligation to limit exchange-rate fluctuations by using the dollar as an intervention currency for spot transactions in the foreign exchange market. The United States, which at the time held about 74 per cent of the world's stock of monetary gold, chose to meet its exchange stability commitment by undertaking to buy and sell gold freely in transactions with monetary authorities at a price related to the parity of the dollar, i.e. $35 an ounce. From time to time parity rates were to be redefined whenever necessary to correct chronic disequilibria in balances of payments. The authors of the Bretton Woods agreements were particularly concerned that exchange-rate changes should take place in an orderly manner and for justifiable reasons. Hence, technically, approval of the IMF was required (for a change of more than 10 per cent from the initial par) and the IMF was supposed to satisfy itself that a 'fundamental disequilibrium' existed in the member country's balance of payments. Fund supervision of parity changes gave expression to the principle that exchange-rate relationships are matters affecting the interests of all.

The second pillar of the system was the arrangement for international liquidity. There was to be a pool of member countries' currencies to be contributed on the basis of a quota system which would enable the IMF to act as a 'lender of last resort' to member countries in temporary balance of payments difficulties. Such assistance was meant to supplement members' own reserves of gold and convertible currencies. In addition quotas could be increased from time to time in order to raise the amount of potential liquidity available to members.

To ensure that these arrangements were maintained the IMF was charged with the responsibility for laying down ground rules for the conduct of international finance, to serve as an instrument of consultation, advice and co-operation between countries. Thus the charter of the IMF provides for exchange controls of short-term capital movements but full freedom for current account transactions. Surplus countries that continually drained foreign exchange reserves from other countries could be discriminated against under the 'scarce currency' clause.[1]

Turning now to the historical evolution of the Bretton Woods system and its problems, we move from the clear-cut world of the conference hall in the summer resort of Bretton Woods to the world of practical reality. The Bretton Woods system never worked quite the way it was intended. Problems developed because of changes in institutions and practices after the war and because countries did not behave as expected. The result was that the post-war international financial system functioned on the basis of a set of arrangements and compromises institutionalised by practice rather than specifically put in place by the Bretton Woods agreements. Specifically, problems arose out of three major changes in economic institutions and practices since 1944:

(1) The expanded use of the dollar as an international currency and a widely accepted reserve asset;

(2) the great increase in the degree of economic interdependence, especially the integration of money markets reflected in the high mobility of capital; and

(3) the comparative rigidity of parity rates that developed in actual practice.

At the end of the Second World War the United States held over 74 per cent of the world's monetary gold stock and accounted for about half of the world's real GNP. Given the economic and financial dominance of the United States it was inevitable that other countries came to regard the U.S. dollar as international money. They used the dollar as an intervention currency to stabilise exchange rates in the market and accumulated it in official reserves. Countries were further prompted in this direction by the failure of gold, a key source of reserves in the Bretton Woods system, to provide a steady and sufficient increase in international liquidity over time. The increase in central banks' demand for gold was greater than the increase in monetary gold stocks resulting from new production because of its artificially low price; the demand could only be met by drawing on U.S. supplies. In the early post-war years of reconstruction the European countries were happy to accumulate dollar balances whenever they could by running balance of payments surpluses with the United States. These funds provided them with access to American commodity and capital markets. The dollar was not merely as good as gold, it was better than gold because dollars (as reserves) earned interest while gold did not. The U.S. deficit after 1958 kept the entire world monetary system liquid. By easing the balance of payments constraint it enabled other individual countries to follow expansive domestic monetary policies and at the same time to continue to build their international reserves. It also allowed European countries to liberalise trade and payments. But while remedying one problem, i.e. the shortage of monetary gold, the steady accumulation of dollars in the hands of foreigners created another serious problem – the deterioration of the international liquidity position of the reserve-currency country, i.e. the reduction in the ratio of U.S. gold stock to U.S. foreign dollar liabilities. Everything depended on the willingness of other countries to go on accumulating dollars in their official reserves – dollars that after the March 1968 two-tier system were largely inconvertible *de facto* into gold.

The system reached an impasse when the United States and the other major industrial countries failed to agree on a resolution of the dilemma faced by the reserve-currency country, the United States. Should the United States seek to achieve external payments balance or permit its deficit to continue in order to provide adequate growth of international reserves? The build-up of largely inconvertible dollar holdings in European and Japanese central banks gradually eroded the credibility of the entire system, which depended in the last analysis on the belief that the dollar's exchange rate was immutable.

The second basic change during the last two decades that transformed the structure of international economic relationships assumed at Bretton Woods was greater economic interdependence and integration. The collapse of the international monetary system might be attributed partly to the increasingly intense clash between an evolutionary trend towards international economic integration on the one hand and the demands of nationalism on the other. In the framing of

economic policies in major countries domestic and international considerations often conflicted. Countries did not
enjoy nearly as much monetary autonomy as had been
expected and desired at Bretton Woods. Starting from the mid-
1950s the world economy was transformed into a transnational
system by the internationalisation of economic activities in
respect of trade, direct investment, portfolio investment, and
short-and medium-term banking operations. The integration
of money markets through institutional developments (Eurocurrency market, multinational corporations, banking con-
sortia, international bond market, etc.) was a striking feature
of the interpendence of national monetary systems. Increased
international mobility of capital, a by-product of the internationalisation of business and banking, was particularly
disruptive to the system. Moving rapidly and massively in
response to interest-rate differentials or anticipations of
exchange-rate changes, volatile capital flows were in large part
responsible for undermining the international monetary order.

A greater threat to the stability of the Bretton Woods system
than the problems associated with increased economic interdependence was the comparative rigidity of parity rates that
developed in actual practice. The presumption gained ground
that the parities of major currencies were not simply pegged but
actually fixed – unlikely to change. This presumption applied
with particular force to the dollar exchange rate. It was
generally assumed that the effective exchange rate of the dollar
would never change, either through a deliberate devaluation
initiated by the United States or by virtue of a general
upvaluation of other important currencies. The excessive
reluctance to change parity values eliminated an effective
means of achieving international adjustment. Par value adjustment decisions were often avoided or postponed by major
trading countries until conditions in financial markets reached
crisis. Except for the 1949 round of adjustments the industrial
countries accounted for fewer than ten exchange-rate changes
during the period 1945–71. Such an attachment to fixed
exchange rates was certainly not anticipated at Bretton Woods.
By the 1960s it was obvious that the international monetary
system had become a disequilibrium system characterised by
persistent deficits and surpluses. More than that, the system

acquired a strongly inflationary bias from the excess creation of international money by the United States, especially after 1965, and the refusal of surplus countries to revalue their currencies. Thus the Bretton Woods system failed to achieve adequate international adjustment and, in addition, laid the groundwork for world inflation.

Despite its manifest shortcomings it would be a mistake to conclude that the Bretton Woods system had been a miserable failure. Compared to the inter-war years a considerable degree of monetary co-operation has occurred under the aegis of the IMF, albeit frequently in smaller groupings of members such as the Group of Ten and the Basle Club. The Fund fostered the habit of international consultation and co-operation in monetary matters. It stood for international monetary order and the reduction of exchange restrictions. However, the system began to totter when it was subjected to entirely new types of economic and political pressures. In practice it depended for its proper functioning on a political relationship between the United States and the other major industrial countries that made the overtones of dollar hegemony acceptable. When this relationship was strained by world inflation emanating from the United States the position of monetary dependence on that country was no longer tolerable to the creditor countries of Europe and Japan, and the pillars crumbled.

5.2 The 1971 Dollar Crisis and its Aftermath

The denouement of the Bretton Woods system was the Dollar Crisis of 1971. We briefly touched on various aspects of this crisis in the preceding chapter, as well as in the foregoing section. Here we analyse the issues more fully in order to provide a backdrop for current discussions of international monetary arrangements.

The crisis stemmed from the U.S. payments deficit. This was an inherent problem of the system in addition to the other sources of strain mentioned in the previous section. For America's trading partners the United States, as the reserve-currency country, was becoming an active inflationary force in the world economy through the continuation of its deficit financed by largely inconvertible dollars. The build-up of dollars in the hands of foreign central banks (as indicated in Table 5.1) inflated the world money supply through expansion of the monetary bases in these countries (see Table 5.2 for

Table 5.1

U.S. Liabilities to Foreign Official Institutions, by Area, 1968–75 (in millions of dollars)

End of period	Total	Western Europe	Canada	Latin America	Asia	Africa	Other countries
1968	17,340	8062	1866	1865	4997	248	302
1969	15,998	7074	1624	1911	4552	546	291
1970	23,775	13,615	2951	1681	4708	407	413
1971	50,651	30,134	3980	1429	13,823	415	870
1972	61,526	34,197	4279	1733	17,577	777	2963
1973	66,827	45,730	3853	2544	10,887	788	3025
1974	76,658	44,185	3662	4419	18,604	3161	2627
1975	79,521	45,139	3137	4448	21,961	2983	1853

Source: Federal Reserve Bulletin (Washington, Feb 1976).

Table 5.2

Growth Rates of Consumer Prices and Money Stock – Six Industrial Countries, 1965–74 (percent change; annual rate)

	Consumer prices		Money stock (M_1)	
Country	1965 to 1970	1970 to 1974	1965 to 1970	1970 to 1974
Canada	3.8	6.4	8.1	19.7
France	4.4	8.0	5.3	12.1
Germany	2.4	6.2	6.4	9.2
Italy	3.0	9.5	15.8	21.9
Japan	5.4	11.0	16.2	24.4
United Kingdom	4.5	10.0	4.1	14.3

Sources: IMF, International Financial Statistics, various issues; OECD, *Main Economic Indicators*.

inflation rates and monetary growth in six industrial countries). For the United States the deficit gave rise to a conflict
between the national and international roles of the dollar
which the United States could not unilaterally resolve without
disrupting the world's monetary system. What the crisis did,
therefore, was to underline the need in any viable monetary
system for a currency unit for monetary reserves that is
sufficiently stable in value and has features that make it a
confident reserve asset. Until 1965 the official view in Washington was that the U.S. payments deficit was better understood
in terms of the foreign demand for international money than as
a consequence of dollar overvaluation. The U.S. government
therefore adopted a policy of 'benign neglect' of its external
payments position and supported proposals for inter-
nationally-created reserve assets, i.e. Special Drawing
Rights (SDRs). But 'benign neglect' was a misleading policy,
for already in 1964 dollar balances held by foreign monetary
authorities equalled the total gold holdings of the United
States. There was a decline in the willingness of private
foreigners to hold additional dollar deposits (or dollar claims)
above minimum levels which, at times, developed into a
speculative demand for gold fuelled by rumours of a possible
devaluation of the dollar in terms of gold. Between 1965 and
1968 an estimated $3000m. worth of gold was sold by central
banks to private speculators. The 1967–8 gold crisis provided
an ideal opportunity for a real adjustment process to begin
through negotiated changes in the existing pattern of exchange
rates, including an increase in the dollar price of gold. Instead
of negotiating on this score the Americans got the Europeans
to accept the establishment of a two-tier gold market in March
1968. This arrangement separated the private gold market
from the official market in which central banks buy and sell
gold to each other. The price of gold in the private market
might rise above $35 an ounce, but the central banks continued
to deal in gold with each other at this fixed price. The largest
surplus country in Europe, Germany, also accepted an American request not to demand conversion of its dollar surplus. In
effect the Europeans accepted in 1968 a *de facto* inconvertible
dollar standard.

Why in 1968 did not the United States then take action to

correct the deficit through currency realignments? U.S. officials believed that because of the asymmetrical role of the dollar they could not correct the dollar's overvaluation by a straightforward exchange-rate adjustment. The devaluation option, available to other countries in 'fundamental disequilibrium', was closed to the United States because the dollar was convertible into gold at $35 an ounce and all the other currencies were tightly pegged to the dollar by government intervention in the foreign exchange markets. That is to say, the exchange rate for the dollar, in contrast to the exchange rates of other national currencies, was not, under the old system, under the unilateral control of the United States. The rate for the dollar was determined by each foreign government fixing the exchange rate for its national currency by intervening in its foreign exchange market with dollars. This is referred to as the 'Nth' currency problem. If there are N countries with N currencies, there can be no more than $N-1$ independently determined exchange rates or prices between these currencies. One of these countries must be passive with respect to the exchange rate of its currency. The dollar, because of its international role, was the 'Nth' currency under the old system. The only way the United States could change its exchange rate was by changing the dollar price of gold; but U.S. officials asserted that this would accomplish nothing because all other countries would follow the dollar – leaving the structure of exchange rates unchanged. In addition they felt that such action would have destroyed the dollar–gold international currency system, increased the role of gold and would have had disruptive effects in many countries. With exchange-rate changes not feasible the only recourse for the United States lay in adjusting domestic economic conditions to produce the desired external balance; this the Americans were unwilling to do. Instead, inflation steadily increased in the United States owing to the excessive monetary expansion in 1965 and 1968 which financed the acceleration of the war in Vietnam. The failure to accompany the monetary growth with a deflationary fiscal policy sufficient to cope with the increased level of demand generated expectations of further inflation. Throughout the period 1966–9 American industries suffered a loss of competitiveness from inflation, so that by 1970 it was clear that domestic demand management was not going to end the deficit.

When the suspension of dollar convertibility came in August 1971 it was in response to overwhelming market pressures, i.e. the speculative movement of funds out of dollars into other major currencies. European countries and Japan had no choice but to float their currencies because of the massive flight of funds into their markets and the impossibility of knowing what new parities would halt the speculation. This alternative – the floating of the surplus currencies, or strictly, under IMF rules, revaluation – although formally open to Europe and Japan was effectively blocked owing to the failure of these countries and the United States to agree on equilibrium parity changes based on the understanding that, should the United States devalue, the other countries would not follow with competitive devaluations. The very same adjustments were made at the Smithsonian Institution meeting in December 1971, but only after a major crisis had developed. The United States increased the dollar price of gold by 8 per cent. The Japanese yen was revalued by 17 per cent and the German mark by 14 per cent. Currencies were allowed to fluctuate within a wider 2.25 per cent range on either side of the newly-fixed rates (called 'central rates').

However, these arrangements were short-lived. Renewed speculative activity in 1972 and early 1973 forced most major countries to abandon fixed rates. The Common Market countries – except the United Kingdom and Italy – embarked on a joint float of their currencies *vis-à-vis* the U.S. dollar. Monetary authorities did not, however, allow their currency values to be determined solely by demand and supply, but intervened from time to time to keep the exchange rates within desired limits. A managed floating rate system has been in operation since then. Floating rates have worked much better than had been initially predicted or feared. Indeed, fortunately for the world economy, they were in use when the oil price rise came along in the autumn of 1973. While relationships between currencies changed markedly (as was to be expected from the upheaval) there was an absence of the disruptions in foreign exchange markets, sudden massive flights of capital and near-panic reactions to reserve losses that characterised the declining years of the fixed rate system when confronted by lesser pressures. In addition, the flexibility of exchange rates permits countries to pursue more independent monetary policies, especially at a time when governments are confronted with the need to fight inflation and high unemployment simultaneously. However, some observers see dangers inherent in the present managed floating arrangements. These are the hazards of competitive depreciations and of proliferation of mutually damaging restrictions on trade and capital flows reminiscent of the 1930s. These risks have been lessened somewhat since June 1974 when floating rates became subject to IMF guidelines defining permissible limits on the management of rates. But the guidelines are defined in rather general terms and their observance is difficult to monitor. Recognising that parities and exchange controls have become politicised to a degree unimaginable only a few years ago, individual countries could drift into a state of continual conflict over exchange rates. Perhaps these dangers are exaggerated, but it makes the task of constructing a new monetary order all the more urgent.

5.3 Perspectives on International Monetary Reform

The subject of international monetary reform is not a new one. Since the late 1950s economists have debated the shortcomings of the system and have proposed a plethora of solutions to the interconnected problems of liquidity, confidence and adjustment. The system itself showed some capacity for evolutionary adaptation through *ad hoc* arrangements, improvisations, political compromises, etc., often dictated by the logic of events, i.e. currency crises. Academic debates were reflected in policy discussions and in the international negotiations for modifications to the system. The notable modifications were the introduction of Special Drawing Rights (SDRs) in 1970, the establishment of the two-tier gold market in 1968 and the 1970 memorandum of the IMF Executive Directors calling for smaller and more frequent adjustment of exchange parities.

The political compromises that resulted in adaptations to the system reflected the fact that national authorities differed in their preferred remedies for specific problems. In view of the fact that the technical aspects of the system have been thoroughly analysed and debated, and that the system has shown some capacity for evolutionary adaptation, it is obvious that conflicting national interests will guarantee a reformed system only slightly different from the previous one. Because the new system has to be built on the basis of political compromise it is unlikely to be radical. The new agreement is, however, sure to include some adaptations and innovations designed to strengthen the adjustment process. The major question that must be resolved or compromised in any viable reform proposal is: How should exchange adjustments occur? This involves agreement on (*a*) the degree of flexibility in exchange rates and (*b*) the role of reserve assets and their interconvertibility.

These issues have been thoroughly debated in the reform negotiations that began in 1972, initially in a Committee of the Board of Governors of the IMF – the Committee of Twenty – and latterly in the Interim Committee, which began work in 1974. In addition to serving as the forum for the final stages in the efforts to obtain agreement on a new international monetary system the Interim Committee is also expected to advise the Board of Governors on the supervision, management and adaptation of the new system. Already the broad outlines of a new monetary system is taking shape. Predictably the choice of exchange-rate system has given rise to the greatest controversy and debate. Otherwise, agreement has been reached on such issues as the role of gold, the future reserve base of the system and the obligations of members of the IMF to collaborate with the Fund in the interests of exchange stability, orderly exchange arrangements and adjustments.

On the question of the future exchange-rate system, differences of view range from those countries that desire a return to fixed parities and those that prefer to see flexibility of exchange rates built into the system. Although leading economists and economic liberals have long advocated a system of freely floating exchange rates there is little support among national authorities for free floating as a permanent feature of the system. In deciding on the choice of exchange-rate regime for an international monetary system a government naturally tends to favour a system that combines safeguards against disruptive actions by other governments in the future with provisions guaranteeing its own freedom of action. Appraising an exchange-rate system on this basis, governments tend to prefer a system with a set of binding rules to one that relies on the market or the price system, i.e. floating exchange rates. Governments generally have a natural reluctance, except in exceptional circumstances, to let exchange rates be determined by markets which they do not control.

It was these attitudes that led the reform committee to recommend a formula that referred to 'stable but adjustable par values and the floating of currencies in particular situations' subject to appropriate rules and surveillance by the Fund. In the negotiations France has been the champion of exchange-rate fixity, while the United States argued for members' freedom to float. The precise form of the future par value system is still to be determined, but support has been growing for a system of 'crawling peg' or 'gliding parities' under which changes in parities would be frequent (as often as once a month), but at the same time limited to a small annual magnitude, e.g. 2 per cent. Controversy exists over the extent to which governments should be compelled to change, or restrained from changing the exchange parity. The alternatives range from a compulsory formula based on an average of past changes in reserves or market exchange rates to total discretion for individual governments. Earlier in the reform discussions the United States supported the former alternative by stressing the need for objective indicators, more automaticity and symmetrical treatment of surplus and deficit countries. The objective indicator, e.g. excessive gains or losses of foreign exchange reserves, would signal the need for a policy change by the country concerned. If adopted, such a scheme would lead to an increase in the frequency and degree of automaticity in adjustment of exchange parities. Given that the reformed system will be one in which the authorities fix the permissible band of variations of the exchange rate around some fixed parity, the authorities must possess international reserves of foreign exchange to support the officially determined rate.

This brings us to the second main feature of a new international monetary system: What is to be the unit for monetary reserves? What should replace the dollar? International monetary systems are often classified by their principal reserve asset or assets – as the gold standard, the gold exchange standard, the dollar standard. The reformed system is to be the SDR standard. The experience of the last fifteen years has shown that countries are reluctant to hold a dominant portion of their international reserves in a form, i.e. U.S. dollars, which they expect to devalue in real terms in the future. In addition, it has been said that the United States had a privileged position in the old system because it could settle payments deficits by adding to its liabilities instead of drawing down its reserve assets. This asymmetry is to be excluded in the reformed system. Countries would keep the great bulk of their reserves in internationally controlled SDRs. Whether any minimum working dollar balances were held by central banks would depend on the extent to which the dollar continued to be used as a market intervention currency. Modest dollar holdings by central banks would not be inconsistent with an SDR standard. All national currencies, including the U.S. dollar, would define their exchange rates in terms of SDRs. The United States would thus be on the same footing as other countries. Dollars which came into the hands of foreign commercial or central banks would automatically be converted into SDRs at the U.S. Federal Reserve. U.S. payments deficits would be financed completely with reserve assets. An SDR standard would solve the Nth currency problem – it would permit as many independent exchange rates to exist as there are currencies.

The SDR facility was originally conceived in the 1960s as a supplement to international liquidity. The scheme had the backing of the United States and the developing countries in opposition to the European pressure for an increase in the official price of gold. SDRs are a form of international money – colloquially referred to as 'paper gold' – and represent a net surplus to the system without a corresponding deficit. They are allocated to IMF members on the basis of their quotas in the Fund and are regarded as owned reserves. When the first allocation was made in 1970, however, the situation had changed from one of shortage to one of excess liquidity. Nevertheless $10,000m. worth of SDRs were distributed to

Fund members between 1970 and 1972. This net addition to international liquidity came at a time when total international reserves were increasing at a rapid rate, i.e. over 50 per cent in the period 1969–71 – from $78,000m. to $130,000m. The inflationary implication of SDR growth is, therefore, one of the problems that has to be tackled in the reform discussions. There are additional problems in connection with the evolution towards an SDR standard. First, how can central banks be induced to hold a significant share of reserves in the form of SDRs? It is not sufficient merely to change the IMF Articles of Agreement making SDRs rather than gold the *de jure* currency. The world would continue to be on a dollar standard as long as the dollar remains the *de facto* international currency. Central bank intervention in the foreign exchange market would have to be switched from dollars to SDRs. This would require that commercial banks also actually hold working balances of SDRs. SDRs would need positive promotion to encourage central banks, commercial banks and others to make substantial changes in their working practices. Second, an SDR system requires that an end be put to free choice in the composition of reserves: otherwise the system would be unstable. Existing reserve currency holdings would therefore have to be consolidated into SDRs at some time in the future.

Some progress has been made towards the objective of making SDRs the central reserve asset of the future. In 1975 agreement was reached on measures designed to reduce the role of gold – 'that barbarous relic', as Keynes called it – in the monetary system, thereby enhancing the status of SDRs. IMF members agreed to abolish the official price of gold and to do away with all requirements for countries to use gold in official dealings with the Fund. One-sixth of the Fund's 150 million ounces stockpile of gold would be sold at free market prices, the profits going to LDCs; another one-sixth of the Fund's gold would be returned to those members that originally contributed it. Since July 1974 the Fund has been valuing SDRs in terms of sixteen currencies instead of the U.S. dollar, as it previously had done. This is expected to give the SDR a higher degree of stability than belongs to any single currency in a floating-rate world. The rate of interest on SDRs was also increased from 1½ per cent to 5 per cent, thereby increasing their attractiveness for central bankers. In the last couple of years some countries have begun to express their exchange rates in SDRs, and its use has spread to commercial transactions. For instance, by 1978 international airlines will quote all fares, rates, etc., in SDRs instead of dollars or sterling, and OPEC countries are likely to adopt an SDR pricing system for oil. As regards the reserve consolidation problem the IMF is considering the establishment of a gold substitution account through which the Fund's members would be able to exchange part or all of their gold holdings for SDRs which would be issued especially for this purpose.

After a protracted period of international negotiation a package of reform measures was agreed in the Interim Committee at its meeting in Jamaica (January 1976). The reforms, in the shape of a proposed amendment to the IMF Articles of Agreement, have to be ratified by national legislatures before the new rules come into force. The ratification process is not likely to be completed before 1978. The proposed amendment, in effect, (*a*) legitimises the greatly increased exchange-rate flexibility which has come into vogue during the past few years while continuing to sanction relatively fixed exchange rates for those countries which prefer them, (*b*) ends the existing system of par values based on gold and (*c*) imposes upon members an obligation to collaborate with the Fund and with each other in order to promote better surveillance of international liquidity and exchange-rate policies of members. However, the replacement of gold and/or reserve currencies by SDRs and, therefore, the effective establishment of the SDR as the principal reserve asset of the system was not agreed and does not form part of the amended Articles. This is not surprising, since SDRs comprise less than 5 per cent of the total reserves of IMF members as compared with gold, which still constitutes 40 per cent of total reserves. The Fund's managing director, Johannes Witteveen, described the new exchange arrangement as providing member countries with 'freedom of choice of exchange arrangements, but not freedom of behaviour'. In other words, each Fund member will be entitled to have the exchange-rate regime of its choice, as long as it does not prevent effective balance of payments adjustment. The executive directors have agreed a document entitled 'Surveillance over Exchange Rate Policies' containing principles and procedures for the 'firm surveillance of exchange rate policies of members'. It prohibits attempts by members to gain an unfair advantage over other members by manipulating exchange rates.

It remains to be seen how these new principles will work out in practice;[2] but for the future one thing is certain we will see the area of collective decision-making enlarged with respect to the adjustment process and the modification of parities. It is evident, however, that IMF members are in no great hurry to adopt the new system until there is a greater degree of monetary stability in the world economy than now exists.

Further Reading

C. A. Coombs, *The Arena of International Finance* (New York: Wiley & Sons, 1976).

H. G. Grubel, *The International Monetary System* (Harmondsworth: Penguin Books, 1971).

G. N. Halm, *A Guide to International Monetary Reform* (Lexington, Mass.: Lexington Books, 1975).

G. M. Meier, *Problems of World Monetary Order* (London and New York: Oxford University Press, 1974).

B. Södersten, *International Economics* (London: Macmillan, 1971) part V contains an excellent analysis of the basic problems of the Bretton Woods System.

R. Solomon, *The International Monetary System, 1945–1976, An Insider's View* (New York: Harper & Row, 1977).

CHAPTER 6

Multinational Corporations

6.1 The Significance of the Multinational Corporation

The growth of direct investment abroad, in particular the rise of the multinational corporation (MNC) has been one of the most significant economic developments of the last two decades. Up to the mid-1960s, the expansion of MNC activity was generally regarded as a favourable trend in the world economy. They were seen as potent agents for economic development through their promotion of a more equitable global distribution of productive capacity, technology, industrial output and income distribution. In the last few years, however, they have come in for a good deal of criticism from many quarters — from organised labour in countries where MNCs are based, by Marxist and neo-Marxist critics, by governments of LDCs. The Marxist critique is the well-known one about 'Big Business' and focuses attention on capitalist State patronage and solicitude for its industrial big battalions — the MNCs. The impact of the MNCs on Third World countries is grist for the mill as a specific area of imperialist muscle-power and ideological conflict. MNCs have been castigated for introducing inappropriate technology in labour-abundant LDCs, the stifling of the growth of local enterprise and for undue interference in national policies. U.S. trade unions have blamed the export of jobs on 'runaway plants' in Mexico, Hong Kong, Taiwan and Korea which operate with cheap labour and efficient American technology, which, they alleged, jeopardise the traditionally high standard of living of American workers;[1] and there were calls for stringent controls on all U.S. direct investment activities. British trade unionists demanded similar curbs on the export of capital for fear of losing factories and jobs to other European countries consequent upon Britain's entry to the E.E.C. Well-publicised isolated stories of MNC

involvement in political intrigue and scandals have not improved the image of the international business giants. The
groundswell of the recent criticism of MNCs was J.-J. Servan-
Schreiber's book *The American Challenge*[2] which, while port-
raying the relative backwardness of European entrepreneurs,
pointed to dangers arising from the acquisition by American
MNCs of dominant control over the high-technology sectors
of the European economy on which it depended for future
growth.

This mounting uneasiness and concern over the trend
towards international business culminated in an enquiry by a
Group of Eminent Persons sponsored by the United Nations.
The defenders of the MNC who feel that the MNCs have been
unfairly maligned have been able to put their views to the
Group, whose report,[3] published in 1974, recognised the
positive benefit of MNCs, but recommended multilateral
control of the system of international production fashioned by
these corporations.

What, then, is a multinational corporation? As is often the
case with novel and controversial phenomena, there is no
agreed definition of what counts as a multinational corporation. Different writers refer variously to 'international',
'transnational' and 'global' corporations (or firms, enterprises
and companies). Obviously, what is meant is a corporation
that controls production facilities in more than one country,
such facilities having being acquired through the process of
foreign direct investment. Firms that participate in international business, however large they may be, solely by
exporting or by licensing technology are not multinational. To
clarify the definition of a multinational corporation it is useful
to distinguish four degrees of involvement in international
operations open to business firms:

(1) export activity
(2) foreign licensing and joint venture
(3) overseas operations and
(4) multinational operations.

These forms of involvement in international marketing and
production reflect increasing degrees of control over the firm's

operations in foreign countries. Export activity is familiar and needs no further comment. Foreign licensing is usually resorted to when (*a*) the firm feels it cannot risk a full-scale entry, (*b*) foreign markets are of limited size, or (*c*) there are restrictions against foreign investment in overseas markets (as in Japan during the 1950s and 1960s). When these conditions prevail the firm may select a local producer to manufacture and market under a licensing agreement. Joint ventures with local companies may be undertaken when condition (*c*) above applies (as in some East European countries) and also when the operation is of such a size that the resources of two or more companies are required, e.g. oil and petrochemicals. Through licensing and joint-venture agreements the firm can usually exercise greater control over marketing in the overseas market than by export activity. Even greater control over the firm's operations is achieved when the firm's products are sold through local distribution subsidiaries or manufactured locally (overseas operations). The firm achieves the status of MNC when it engages in production and marketing (through subsidiaries) in several countries on such a scale that its fortunes rest in more than one country and its management adopts a multinational strategy. Some analysts define a MNC as a corporation deriving more than 25 per cent of its profits (sometimes sales) from production and marketing in foreign countries. Vernon[4] limits the term to firms that control operations in at least six countries. In terms of this definition he found 187 U.S. firms that fitted this description in 1971. He regards the MNC as a company that attempts to carry out its activities on an international scale, as though there were no national barriers, on the basis of a common management strategy directed from the corporate centre. It should be noted, however, that not all MNCs adopt a highly centralised integrated production or marketing strategy towards their affiliates; there are many instances where MNCs treat their foreign affiliates as autonomous units. Control of production facilities abroad may stem from majority ownership of the foreign firm's equity capital; frequently, less than majority ownership of the equity is sufficient to ensure effective control if the ownership of shares are widely held.

Though 'bigness' is characteristic of MNCs, like nation-

states, they come in many different shapes and sizes, have
different management and distinctive corporate identities,
pursue different interests and operate in varying market
conditions often in competition with each other. They are not
all programmed like monolithic robots fanning out from their
respective countries of origin with a common set of in-
structions. There are between 500 and 700 MNCs (depending
on the definition used) operating in the world today. Half of
them are U.S. multinationals, the rest are based outside the
United States. The bulk of foreign direct investment associated
with multinational business activity is accounted for by a
relatively small number of MNCs; for instance, fifty of the
largest MNCs accounted for half the total international direct
investment and a higher proportion of international production in 1971. The 187 U.S. multinational firms identified by
Vernon presently account for around 80 per cent of U.S.
foreign direct investment and over half of all U.S. exports of
manufactured goods. In terms of value added, production by
all MNCs now exceeds 20 per cent of total world GNP,
excluding the centrally planned economies. In over twenty
countries MNCs currently account for over one-third of the
output of manufacturing industries. The production of each of
the ten leading MNCs is greater than the national incomes of
eighty independent countries. Over 60 per cent of trade in
manufactures among the developed countries is carried on by
MNCs, a large proportion of which is sales of components,
finished products, etc. (i.e. transfers between the parent
corporations and their subsidiaries). The U.S. Commerce
Department estimated in 1970 that 25 per cent of American
manufactured exports reflected this intra-firm trade. A few
MNCs in the non-socialist world are state-owned; twelve of
them are included in the 1973 U.N. report's list of 211 leading
manufacturing MNCs with sales of over $1000m. With the
increasing trend towards greater State intervention in industry
in many countries we are likely to see more state-owned
MNCs. Regional integration among LDCs will also nourish
the growth of MNCs in the more advanced LDCs. There is also
a growing number of socialist-owned MNCs in the countries of
Eastern Europe (around fifty in 1975). Although their sphere of
operations is largely within COMECON, they have a number

of subsidiaries and associates in Western capitalist countries as well as in the LDCs.

Table 6.1 provides the most recent investment information available on a relatively comparable basis. The data are reported in terms of book value which understate the current or market value. If the data are adjusted for accrued value the total for 1971 could easily reach $250,000m. A two-to-one relationship is usually assumed to exist between output and asset values. Applying this ratio to the $165,000m. of direct investment the total value of international production (defined as sales by foreign affiliates of MNCs to non-affiliates) associated with MNCs would appear to be at least $330,000m.

Table 6.1

Stock of Foreign Direct Investment (book value) held by Major Countries 1967 and 1971

	1967		1971	
Country	Millions of $	% share	Millions of $	% share
United States	59,486	55.0	86,001	52.0
United Kingdom	17,521	16.2	24,019	14.5
France	6000	5.5	9540	5.8
West Germany	3015	2.8	7276	4.4
Switzerland	4250	3.9	6760	4.1
Canada	3728	3.4	5930	3.6
Japan	1458	1.3	4480	2.7
Netherlands	2250	2.1	3580	2.2
Sweden	1514	1.4	3450	2.1
Italy*	2110	1.9	3350	2.0
Belgium*	2040	0.4	3250	2.0
Australia*	380	1.9	610	0.4
Portugal*	200	0.2	320	0.2
Denmark*	190	0.2	310	0.2
Norway*	60	0.0	90	0.0
Austria*	30	0.0	40	0.0
Other	4000	3.7	6000	3.6
Total	108,200	100.0	165,000	100.0

Source: *Multinational Corporations in World Development* (New York: United Nations, 1973).

NOTE:* Data on book value of foreign direct investment are only available for LDCs.

What is the explanation for this trend towards multinational business? What are the motives for investing abroad? Why do firms go beyond exporting and the licensing of foreign firms? Several theoretical explanations have been offered in the last ten years. Most of them are variants on a central theme: the firms that go multinational are those with some kind of monopoly advantage that is best exploited by maintaining management control of operations in foreign countries. According to these theories foreign direct investment occurs in industries characterised by oligopolistic market structures in both home and foreign countries. This oligopolistic market environment, conducive to foreign investment, is one in which each individual firm enjoys monopolistic profits through possessing and controlling some type of firm-specific, rent-yielding advantages. These advantages may be a superior product or production process, lower costs of production owing to economies of scale or preferential access to capital or raw materials; or a differentiated product promoted through advertising or simply superior management skills or, indeed, a combination of all these advantages. However, the foreign firm is usually at a disadvantage compared with local firms because of its unfamiliarity with local market conditions, i.e. the firm contemplating foreign investment must reckon with higher information costs. Therefore the possession of some advantage is a necessary condition for foreign direct investment if the foreign firm is to meet the competition of local firms which are close to the market and have familiar lines of communication, including distribution links. And, indeed, the evidence indicates that technological advantages resulting from heavy expenditure in research and development (R & D) are highly correlated with foreign direct investment. Marxists and radical critics dispute this account for the spread of multinational business and argue instead that foreign investment is an institutional necessity for corporate capitalism in the West, stemming from the need for an outlet for surplus capital generated in such capitalist economies. To confuse (or, perhaps, clarify!) matters further John Kenneth Galbraith[5] emphasises the unique organisational characteristics of modern big business as important determinants of foreign direct investment in addition to the existence of an oligopolistic market environment. The control of these giant corporations is in the hands of a technical-managerial class, not the shareholders, who play a purely passive role. This managerial class (the 'technostructure') strives for security by eliminating uncertainties in the market both at home and abroad through controlling those who supply goods and services to the corporation as well as the consumers of its products. The technostructure is, in effect, a planning system that willy-nilly impels the large corporation into overseas marketing and production for security and continued growth.

Turning from general hypotheses to the evidence from industry case studies we find a variety of motives for international investment. The following are typical:

(1) A need to get behind tariff walls to safeguard a company's export market against the emergence of local competition (getting behind the E.E.C.'s common external tariff was certainly a major consideration for U.S. companies during the last fifteen years).

(2) Greater efficiency and responsiveness by producing in the local market as compared with exporting to it.

(3) The possibility of lower production costs (especially labour costs) abroad prompting the production of components, etc., in low-wage countries.

(4) As a defensive measure to forestall efforts by competitors to capture lucrative foreign markets and to keep open sources of supply.

(5) The need to diversify product lines to avoid fluctuations in earnings.

(6) The desire to exploit technological advantages more fully by setting up production units abroad than by licensing foreign firms, especially when markets are expanding and capital is readily available.

(7) A desire to avoid home-country regulations, e.g. antitrust legislation in the United States.

The motives for international investment in petroleum and mining are quite clear. These are by nature international industries and the sources of supply are located abroad. To develop these resources companies have had to set up in-

ternational production, refining and marketing facilities overseas. In the manufacturing field MNCs tend to be concentrated
in the high-technology, research-intensive industries and those
characterised by oligopolistic market structures. For instance,
U.S. multinationals control 80 per cent of computers and more
than 90 per cent of microcircuit production in the E.E.C. And,
indeed, it is quite apparent that international production does
not take place in any significant volume in standardised goods
produced by competitive industries such as textiles, clothing,
flour milling, etc. But there are some important low-technology
industries where multinational firms flourish, e.g. food products, soft drinks, motor-cars, cosmetics. On the other hand,
multinational companies are noticeably absent in certain
industries that are both oligopolistically organised and technologically advanced, e.g. steel and aircraft. The reason is
probably that in many countries such industries are subject to
state ownership or control. Clearly the existence of market
imperfections, in particular, branding, advertising and product
differentiation, and not necessarily oligopolistic structures,
provides the most fertile field for multinational business
activity.

Much of the research, both theoretical and empirical, has
concentrated on the behaviour of U.S. multinationals; but in
recent years the scope has been widened to include the activities
of MNCs based outside the United States. From the mid-1960s
European and Japanese multinationals increased their operations at a more rapid pace than U.S. firms; and it is therefore
pertinent to consider the pattern of this growth to see in what
respects it is consistent with, or differs from, the traditional
stereotype based largely on U.S. multinational experience.
European multinationals, like their U.S. counterparts, are to
be found in oligopolistic markets, but they tend to derive their
multinational business advantage less from product innovation than from process innovation and the development of
synthetics. In addition, relying less on superior management
skills, European firms expanded overseas mainly to overcome
tariff and non-tariff barriers in foreign markets. The rise of
Japanese multinationals was particularly dramatic: between
1960 and 1971 Japanese overseas direct investment increased
from $300m. to $4500m., a fifteen-fold increase. Table 6.2

Table 6.2

Distribution of Japan's Foreign Direct Investment by Industrial Sector and Region (in millions of U.S. dollars and percentage end 1973)

Region	Extractive sector	Manufacturing sector	Commerce and services
North America	272 (9.4)*	550 (18.7)	1,453 (43.1)
Europe	47 (1.6)	138 (4.7)	924 (27.4)
Latin America	204 (7.1)	932 (31.8)	479 (14.2)
Asia	692 (23.9)	1,096 (37.4)	400 (11.9)
Oceania	394 (13.7)	150 (5.1)	84 (2.5)
Middle East	1,158 (40.1)	26 (0.8)	9 (0.3)
Africa	119 (4.1)	41 (1.4)	22 (0.7)
Total	2,886 (100.0)	2,933 (100.0)	3,371 (100.0)

Source: Japanese Ministry of International Trade and Industry, *Tsusho Hakusho* (White Paper on International Trade) (Tokyo, 1974).
* Figures in brackets show percentages.

shows the industrial and regional distribution of Japanese overseas investment in 1973. A unique feature of Japanese overseas investment is its heavy concentration in commerce and services (36.7 per cent of total Japanese foreign direct investment).[6] These are marketing operations consisting of distributive outlets, advertising, sales promotion and after-sales services. They were set up to handle the phenomenal increase in Japanese exports of cars, motor cycles, radios and TV sets during the 1960s. They account for the bulk of Japanese investment in the developed countries. In 1973 63.8 per cent of total Japanese direct investment in the United States was in such fields, and 83.3 per cent in the E.E.C. Equally distinctive, but not surprising for a resource-deficient country,

Japan devotes a larger proportion of its total foreign direct investment to the extractive sector than other countries (36.8 per cent compared with 35 per cent for the United States and 7.2 per cent for the United Kingdom). Such investment is aimed at securing adequate and stable supplies of fuels and raw materials for home-market industries. The Japanese have consequently been competing for scarce oil facilities in the Middle East and Indonesia and copper ore and bauxite wherever they can acquire ownership rights. Japanese multinational business operations in LDCs (mainly in South-East Asia and Latin America) consist in the manufacturing of labour-intensive low-technology products for sale in local and third-country markets. A notable feature of the spread of Japanese multinationals has been the active involvement of the state in planning, guiding and assisting foreign direct investment through the Ministry of International Trade and Industry (MITI). This, of course, is just one instance of the generally closer collaboration between industry and government in Japan than found elsewhere in Western countries.

6.2 Multinationals and Development

According to the supporters of MNCs the world economy derives two important benefits from the operations of multinational corporations: the internationalisation of production and the efficient transfer of technology. The two, of course, are related. International production often involves the transfer of technology, and both developments are assisted by the internationalisation of banking and financial services. International production is the share of world output generated by foreign production of multinational corporations. It is measured by the sales of foreign affiliates and subsidiaries of MNCs. The volume of international production thus defined now exceeds conventional trade flows understood as international commerce between independent importers and exporters in different countries. Simply stated, this trend means that production of the world's goods are increasingly being diffused among countries in a pattern that ignores national frontiers. MNCs tend to treat the world as a single integrated market.

They attempt to integrate the operations of their various scattered affiliates so as to achieve least-cost production and subsequent distribution wherever markets exist. The location of plants, investment decisions and the choice of distribution outlets are indeed made by MNCs to maximise corporate returns or on the basis of company advantage generally; but in the process it leads to an efficient world allocation of resources and the maximisation of world welfare (or so it is claimed). In general this is the view of orthodox economists. The reasoning is that, if resources are invested on a global scale where they earn the highest return, then world output would be maximised in a Pareto-optimal sense. When rates of return are equated at the margin, then no further reallocation can make anyone better off without making someone else worse off. But, of course, this is purely an efficiency criterion and offers no guarantee that the resulting income distribution would be desirable in terms of social welfare. Moreover, countries are not particularly interested in the maximisation of global income. They seek to maximise national income and welfare from foreign direct investment in addition to the attainment of other economic and social objectives such as full employment, more equitable distribution of income and national control of domestic resources.

In so far as the MNCs move labour-intensive production facilities to poor countries to take advantage of favourable conditions for process and component specialisation they undoubtedly contribute to greater world efficiency in production.

International manufacturing production involving LDCs really started in the 1960s. In industries where economies of scale were the source of cost advantages to MNCs developing countries' markets were too small to warrant the establishment of manufacturing facilities. In a few isolated cases what production there was was largely for the use of the parent company. Beginning in the early 1960s, as the influences of import substitution policies waned and LDC governments offered generous investment and tax incentives to foreign investors, U.S. multinationals made investments in electronic plants and other simple consumer industries in Korea, Taiwan, Hong Kong, Singapore, Mexico, etc. The added attraction was, of course, lower labour costs. The concentration of production in locations of least cost was powerfully assisted by developments such as containerisation, satellite communications and the general relaxation of trade controls. The processing and assembly of components abroad by U.S. multinationals was encouraged by two relatively obscure provisions in the U.S. tariff schedules (items 806.30 and 807.00) which permit the value of U.S.-made parts to be deducted from the dutiable value of goods imported into the United States. Import duties are thus levied only upon the foreign value added.

The example of U.S. multinationals in developing this new pattern of international production was followed in the 1970s by European and Japanese firms. Spurred by labour shortages and rising labour costs at home, Japanese multinationals are rapidly transferring production facilities to neighbouring South-East Asian countries and Latin America for the manufacture of low-technology, labour-intensive products such as textiles, electrical appliances, radios, etc. Japan no longer derives any particular advantage in the domestic manufacture of these products, hence the move to more favourable overseas areas. In all such manufacturing operations in LDCs a triangular pattern of production and trade is developing. The output is exported back to the parent company or sold in third-country markets. It is a system of international sub-contracting that first started with electronics and textiles, but is now spreading to a wider range of industries such as watchmaking, photographic equipment and other consumer industries.[7]

International production in LDCs has involved a considerable inflow of capital into these countries. In 1968–72 they received $3500m. a year in direct investment, or over 20 per cent of their total capital imports. During the 1960s this flow increased at an average rate of 9 per cent, much of it concentrated in a few developing countries. During the period 1966–9 foreign direct investment in Latin America comprised 60 per cent of total net capital inflow. The stock of foreign direct investment in LDCs increased by about 35 per cent from $35,000m. in 1967 to $47,000m. in 1971. However, for various reasons having to do with the less favourable attitude towards MNCs in some LDCs, growing fears of nationalisation, etc., the LDCs as a group have been losing ground to the developed countries as recipients of direct investment.

Turning to technology transfers, this was a widely acclaimed feature of MNCs in early discussions on the subject. European interest in closing the 'technology gap' with the United States focused attention on the role of the MNC, then predominantly American, in assisting this process. Subsequently it was claimed what U.S. multinationals did for Europe they could do for the LDCs. They could speed up the process of industrialisation through a rapid diffusion of production and managerial technology. Given time, the spread of multinational enterprises would move the world to a closer approximation of the idealised neo-classical model where production technology is equally available to all countries. MNCs provide a package of capital, technology, management and organisational skills. This, it is claimed, is the essence of direct investment. Such technological resources are not available to developing countries from other sources or, if available, only under unfavourable licensing arrangements or through purchase from expensive engineering and management consultants. Complete industrial systems are made available to developing countries, which means new industries, increased employment and higher incomes. In addition MNCs increase human capital formation in such countries through the provision of training opportunities. The evidence indicates that MNCs do provide more technical and managerial training in LDCs than do governments through aid programmes. As far as U.S. manufacturing subsidiaries in LDCs are concerned it has been estimated that less than 10 per cent of managerial staff and about 2 per cent of technical personnel are expatriates.[8] To the extent that multinationals provide greater opportunities for technical and managerial training in LDCs, technology is not merely used in these countries but is also transferred to nationals.

MNCs do make advanced technology available to developing countries, but it is widely felt that the import of foreign technology has not had the positive effect hoped for and claimed. Multinationals are seen as important contributors to the factor proportions problem in developing countries, i.e. they extend and reinforce a labour-saving bias to the industrialisation of these countries. They do this by transferring technology that is appropriate to their home countries, but which is patently ill-suited to the development needs of capital-poor, labour-surplus developing countries. The methods of production are typically capital-intensive and based on long, standardised production runs. The MNC's technology is designed for world-wide profit maximisation, not the development needs of poor countries, in particular employment needs and relative factor scarcities in these countries. In general, it is asserted, the imported technologies are not adapted to (*a*) the consumption needs, (*b*) the size of domestic markets, (*c*) resource availabilities and (*d*) stage of development of many of the LDCs.

Development planners in poor countries fear the adverse effects of technological dependence upon long-term growth. Multinationals produce mainly for the upper middle class (the élite groups) whose tastes are strongly influenced by those prevailing in developed countries; little is therefore done to improve the lot of the poor. Developing countries would like to see a scaling down of production techniques, more labour-intensive methods that might reduce the chronically high unemployment levels in these countries and the manufacture of products designed for low-income consumers.[9] Clearly, LDC dissatisfaction with transferred technology stems from a basic conflict of interest and objectives: LDCs desire the maximisation of employment, an increase in export earnings and long-term social development. The MNCs are interested in maximising corporate earnings. In many cases MNCs have no incentive to adapt production processes to local conditions because their monopoly advantages insulate them from competitive pressures and the necessity of minimising costs. In other instances labour-intensive technique may be resisted because such methods add to production costs or because distortions in factor markets reduce the incentive to use more labour. In many of the industries associated with MNCs alternative labour-intensive techniques do not exist or are inferior in terms of productivity and quality of product. Consequently, it is not unusual to find domestically-owned firms using the same technology as the foreign subsidiaries.

Recently there have been attempts to get at the facts. Do

multinationals adapt technology or not? Are they responsive to local factor endowments and conditions? In particular do they employ more labour and less capital in capital-poor, labour-abundant countries? A recent detailed study of the choice of technology by multinational firms in Brazil found little basis for the assertion that MNCs do not adapt their production processes when they move to a developing country.[10] The evidence suggested that there is a substantial modification of production processes by U.S. multinationals in Brazil. They use one-third to one-fourth as much capital per man as in the United States. The industries included motor vehicles, electrical equipment, household appliances and general industrial machinery. Much of the adaptation resulted from the use of fewer automatic and specialised machines than is the practice in comparable establishments in the United States. Both U.S. and other multinationals use three to four times more labour per unit of capital than in their own home countries in a wide variety of industries; but this was explained in terms of smaller-scale operations in Brazil rather than the existence of lower labour costs. The Brazilian evidence is particularly illuminating because foreign investment is quite large and diverse in the manufacturing sector and multinationals have been involved in the country's development for a longer period than in most LDCs. What the Brazilian experience with MNCs indicates is that foreign firms have the capacity or potential to adapt to LDC conditions, but perhaps they are not as diligent in searching for more labour-intensive techniques as LDC governments might desire. Possibilities of adaptation clearly depend on the type of products. For instance, in the process industries (chemicals, plastics, cement, etc.) the scope for varying factor proportions and production techniques is rather limited and determined mainly by economies of scale and technical considerations. With products for which the cross-elasticity of demand is low and production costs are low relative to selling price, e.g. pharmaceutical products, there is little incentive to adapt technology. On the other hand, where the opposite demand and cost conditions apply, e.g. in domestic appliances and electrical goods, adaptations tend to be extensive with cost-minimisation exerting its influence on the side of labour-intensive techniques.

Much of the earlier research supported the assertion that MNCs do little to adapt technology in capital-poor countries, except for such minor adjustments as the use of more labour and less expensive equipment in assembly operations and materials handling. In a study of the operating characteristics of thirteen U.S. subsidiaries in LDCs Yeoman found that most of them transferred their production processes intact.[11] There was little difference in the amounts of capital per worker in plants located in developed as compared with developing countries. This was especially the case in industries charac- terised by oligopolistic market structures. The same picture emerged from a study of multinationals in Indonesia.[12] However, no systematic bias for or against capital-using techniques was detected in a sample of Japanese and U.S. multinationals in South Korea.[13] A comparison of fourteen United States multinationals with local counterparts in the Philippines and Mexico produced no clear evidence that the MNCs contribute significantly to a capital-using production bias in these countries.[14] It should be pointed out however that in many LDCs domestic firms are to be found employing roughly similar capital/labour ratios as MNCs; but it is maintained that the pace is set by the multinationals in their midst. Technological dependence therefore inhibits local firms from developing their own capabilities for adopting less costly or more labour-intensive production techniques.

MNCs can make an important positive contribution to the foreign exchange earnings of LDCs. With their world-wide production and marketing systems multinationals are able to generate increases in manufactured exports and thus assist poor countries to overcome the foreign exchange constraint on development. But, here again, the evidence is inconclusive on the export performance of MNCs. In South Korea (1970) it has been found that foreign multinationals (U.S. and Japanese) exported a larger proportion of their output than domestic firms; but they also tend to import more and to buy less from Korean firms than Korean firms producing the same product. The products considered were transistors, radios, cotton cloth and yarn, baseball gloves and wigs.[15] In an econometric analysis of MNC export performance in ten Latin American countries Morgenstern and Müller produced results which indicate that the MNCs do export more to Latin America, but not to the rest of the world compared with local firms.[16] This result emerged from tests using aggregated data across all industries. When separate estimates were made for each industry the authors find no evidence that the MNCs export more in any particular industry either to Latin America or the rest of the world. The evidence so far has been derived from small samples in only a few countries; useful generalisations about the export performance of MNCs must therefore await more systematic quantitative analyses of larger samples of firms and countries.

The same caution applies to the question of the prevalence or otherwise of 'transfer pricing' practices by MNCs. Transfer pricing refers to the setting of prices on goods and services bought and sold between a parent company and its foreign subsidiary. Such internal prices do not necessarily correspond with prices established in 'arms-length' transactions, i.e. deals between two independent and unrelated parties where prices are determined by market forces. Overcharging for imports (relative to the international market price) has been documented for Colombia.[17] Subsidiaries of MNCs in the pharmaceutical industry paid 155 per cent more than the c.i.f. price for intermediate drugs (chemical compounds) imported from parent firms. Overcharging to the extent of 40 per cent was also found in the rubber industry, the chemical industry (26 per cent) and in the electronics industry (16–60 per cent). No wonder that such subsidiaries earned no profit and paid no taxes in Colombia! If this practice is as widespread as some believe, then the MNCs use intra-firm sales to transfer profits out of developing countries, especially where LDCs limit dividend repatriation. In addition exports may be underpriced. In a sample of multinational firms operating in Latin America Morgenstern and Müller found evidence which suggested that manufactured exports were underinvoiced to the extent of 40 per cent.[18] The foreign exchange loss for the ten Latin American countries involved was of the order of over $47m. during the late 1960s. Combined with an unknown loss due to overpricing of imports this practice conflicts sharply with the pressing need of these and similar countries to conserve foreign exchange. Why do multinationals manipulate transfer prices?

Why do parent firms overcharge their subsidiaries for imports or oblige them to underprice exports? The answers have to do with the fact that parent firms run their overseas subsidiaries in order to maximise the parent global profits and not necessarily the accounting profits of any particular subsidiary. Thus the parent may discriminate against the more efficient subsidiaries (*a*) to reduce local tax liability (through high transfer prices) or to move profits to a subsidiary in a tax haven[19] (through low transfer prices); in other words, the management of a multinational concern can determine, within limits, its own taxation base, (*b*) to get around restrictions on dividend repatriation, (*c*) to sidestep currency-exchange regulations and to minimise foreign exchange losses from possible devaluations by shifting funds through inflated transfer prices, (*d*) to effect non-reported loans from one subsidiary to another, (*e*) to drain profits out of a subsidiary when the subsidiary faces tough labour negotiations so that the firm can argue that it is not in a position to accede to union demands. The managers of multinational firms admit to a certain amount of arbitrary, or, as they prefer to call it, 'creative', transfer pricing because in many cases there is no market for the goods involved in intra-firm sales, especially where parts and intermediate inputs are the products of expensive firm-specific research, e.g. computer components. It is difficult to know how widespread the practice really is. Multinational firms have an interest in keeping the practice to a minimum from a management accounting perspective as distinct from financial accounting (concerned with taxation, foreign currency cover and overnight balances) because it complicates the problem of evaluating the competitive performance of overseas subsidiaries. In addition the practice creates conflicts between executives of a company in different countries on such matters as morale and managers' incentive bonuses. There are also external checks on the practice, e.g. recent changes in the treatment of tax havens by tax authorities in developed countries have greatly reduced the scope for manipulating intra-firm transfer prices for tax-avoidance purposes. Customs officials are also alerted when they discover the same part or machine arriving at a subsidiary's destination from different sources bearing different prices.

Concern with transfer pricing by MNCs is connected with the question of how to determine the true level of profits earned by these companies on overseas operations. Except in the petroleum industry, the return on investments in the LDCs has not been greater than the return earned in developed countries. According to a U.S. Department of Commerce survey, U.S. multinationals in the manufacturing sector earned a 15.8 per cent rate of return in developing countries compared with 17.9 per cent in developed countries in 1972.[20] Earnings are broadly defined to include profits, interest, royalties and management fees. Rates of return are earnings as percentages of the book value of U.S. investment. Some analysts claim that these figures disguise and understate the true profit earned by MNCs in LDCs because of the large additional earnings from the overpricing of imports and underpricing of exports. The profits of U.S.-based manufacturing enterprises in Latin America during the 1960s have been estimated at around 40 per cent. According to one reckoning, pharmaceutical subsidiaries in that region earned an average rate of return in the 1960s of 79.1 per cent, including overpricing of imports but excluding export underpricing.[21]

Despite a feeling of dissatisfaction with the role of MNCs in contributing to economic and social development in poor countries there also exists a recognition by policy-makers in these countries that given adequate safeguards LDCs can capture the benefits of direct investment without the evils. The next section examines changing attitudes towards MNCs.

6.3   Policies towards Multinationals

Attitudes and policies are changing almost everywhere towards MNCs. In many parts of the world they are not as freely welcomed as they once were; in some countries severe restrictions are placed on their operations, including agreed divestiture and nationalisation. Attitudes were different in the 1950s and early 1960s. Then, governments in developed and underdeveloped countries vied with each other to attract direct investment by indiscriminately granting tax incentives, subsidies, free plant sites, low-cost loans, government procurement contracts and tariff protection. In the developed countries such incentives were usually provided to help depressed regions overcome unemployment problems. In LDCs the encouragement of foreign direct investment was part of import-substitution industrialisation strategies. But partly as a result of increased knowledge about the characteristics of foreign investors and increasing scepticism about their role as engines of development governments in LDCs are counting the costs of inward direct investment. The emphasis is shifting towards control and away from positive encouragement in order to appropriate the benefits while lessening the cost. The aim is to channel foreign investment flows into activities where the marginal social benefits are highest relative to the costs. Recognising that they are dealing with powerful international oligopolies, national authorities are devising policies to improve their bargaining position in relation to MNCs. Control and regulations are taking many forms, but the basic desire is to screen investment projects and accept only those consistent with the host country's economic and social priorities. This usually means investments which (*a*) increase foreign exchange earnings, (*b*) increase significantly the employment of local labour, (*c*) involve local-capital participation and (*d*) reduce the costs of some important necessity.

The conditions under which technology is transferred through corporate ownership and control is one area of conflict. LDCs would like to untie the package of technology, skills, management and marketing know-how. They wish to obtain the basic ingredients through other mechanisms – for instance, joint ventures, licensing or management contracts. These arrangements, it is felt, decrease technological dependence and can help develop indigenous technical and entrepreneurial capabilities. The countries in the Andean Common Market (Bolivia, Chile, Colombia, Ecuador, Peru and Venezuela) have introduced new procedures and guidelines[22] on foreign investment and transfer of technology that are among the most comprehensive in the Third World. Limitations are placed on the amounts of royalty payments that subsidiaries as well as local firms can pay for imported technology. This is to prevent competition by local firms for technology as well as to check overpricing and the draining of profits from the developing countries involved. The most stringent regulation concerns the disinvestment of assets – the so-called 'fade-out' regulation. Under this clause multinational firms must sell majority holdings of the established subsidiary assets to local investors, and new foreign investors must take minority positions within a fifteen-year period in order to be eligible for trade concessions within the Andean Common Market. The only exception to this rule is the case of foreign firms that export a high proportion of their output. The intention is to turn multinational operations in these countries into joint ventures. Joint ventures are attractive to developing countries because they enable local investors (usually governments) to share in the quasi-rents (monopoly or oligopoly profits) earned by foreign firms. Vertically integrated foreign firms are, however, reluctant to enter into joint-venture agreements because they thereby lose control of part of their technological and marketing advantages. The viability of joint ventures is also threatened by differences between partners of unequal economic strength over such matters as the expected rate of return, the proportion of earnings to be ploughed back, dividends, etc. From the multinational corporation's point of view, however, there is one advantage in a phased joint venture, and that is that the firm retains control of the enterprise during the early years. MNCs have been exploring different investment techniques in recent years, in particular the experience of Western multinationals in Eastern Europe shows that firms can devise various structures that meet the requirements of countries desirous of obtaining entrepreneurial skills and technology but are sensitive to perpetual and highly visible foreign ownership. An example of new modes of co-operation now being developed by multinationals to meet the requirements of host countries is the $7m. ITT investment in a satellite earth communications station in Indonesia. Having financed and built the facility, ITT agreed to hand over the assets to the government of Indonesia in exchange for a contract to operate and manage the station on the basis of a 50/50 split in earnings. Foreign investment in LDC resource development is never popular in the host countries. It has led to serious political wrangles and confrontations in almost every country. As a result of political tensions and uncertainties, investment has been diverted in recent years to production of higher-cost raw materials in industrial countries. For instance, despite the boom in commodity markets, U.S. investment abroad (new and reinvested earnings) in mining and smelting in 1972–3 was almost 20 per cent less than the average for the previous five years; in real terms the reduction was even greater.[23] This trend is neither in the interests of developed countries concerned at the rising real cost of resource production nor those of developing countries interested in the promotion of local processing of raw materials. One solution to the problem that deserves the support of other capital-exporting countries is the U.S. proposal for the establishment of an international institution to facilitate new methods of financing and participation with foreign investors and host governments in resource projects. An institution like the International Finance Corporation of the World Bank (with increased capital resources) can perform this function. The IFC can help protect the interests of LDCs in formulating the terms of ventures and can temporarily take an equity share for ultimate resale to local investors.

The Japanese example is frequently cited as an indication of how an industrialising country can acquire modern technological capabilities through channels other than foreign ownership and control such as licensing. However, technological absorptive capacity in most LDCs is not equal to the task of adapting foreign technology, mainly due to the lack of financial and skilled manpower resources. In addition, it is by no means certain that domestic production under foreign licence or management contract is less costly than direct investment. Joint ventures, too, are often subject to more restrictions on exports and involve higher payments for technology than wholly-owned subsidiaries.[24]

Two-thirds of direct investment takes place in the developed countries. In these countries, too, current policy is towards greater control and surveillance pragmatically applied. Industrial policy in the E.E.C. is designed to encourage mergers between European companies so as to provide more equal competition to U.S. multinationalists in the Common Market. This is supported by recent moves towards a common technological policy among member countries. In 1976 the OECD countries agreed a voluntary code of conduct for multi-nationals which, among other things, requires maximum disclosure of information by such firms. The Common Market Commission is at present engaged in drawing up a list of 'fair' transfer prices in the E.E.C. When completed it would provide a reference check against actual prices quoted by companies. Such information would be useful to tax and other regulatory authorities having dealings with multinational companies. Section 482 of the U.S. Inland Revenue Code gives the American tax authorities discretion to reconstruct intra-firm transfer prices to ensure that corporations pay their fair share of U.S. taxes. Canada, which has attracted relatively more foreign direct investment than any other country, has long been concerned with the effects of multinational firms on the Canadian economy. Recently (1973) a Foreign Investment Review Agency (FIRA) was established to review take-overs and investment by new or established foreign-based firms in new lines of business. Among the criteria adopted by the Agency for approving a new foreign direct investment are compatibility with Canadian industrial and economic policies and the degree of Canadian participation in ownership or management of the subsidiary. The Canadian authorities also show a growing preference for joint ventures with private or public Canadian investment.

Some observers believe that to make national policies and regulations effective they must be backed up by international co-operation or parallel action by major countries. Proposals range from the setting up of a 'GATT for direct investment'[25] to the establishment of a U.N. Commission on Multinational Corporations which would work out suitable codes of conduct. The 1974 U.N. report on MNCs came out in favour of a Commission, as well as the adoption of a number of steps including technical assistance designed to strengthen the bargaining position of LDCs *vis-à-vis* multinational firms. These proposals indicate the extent of political attention multinationals are receiving. At the 1976 Nairobi meeting of UNCTAD a Panel of Experts was appointed to work on the draft outlines of a code of conduct with respect to technology transfer and multinational business practices for adoption by the U.N. The question whether such a code will be mandatory or voluntary has not yet been determined. But it is clear that national authorities will continue to adopt different attitudes and policies to MNCs, depending upon their ideological persuasions and perceptions of national interests (foreign direct investment is welcomed and encouraged in South East Asia). It is also clear that the practices of multinationals are as much influenced by the economic policies of host governments as by their profit-seeking goals.

Looking to the future, many analysts now predict a slower rate of growth of multinational investment in the decade of the 1980s and increasing government participation in multinational business projects. The international firms are likely to change their organisational form as they accommodate to increased representation on their management boards of government, labour and consumer groups.

Further Reading

R. J. Barnet and R. E. Müller, *Global Reach: The Power of the Multinational Corporation* (London: Cape, 1975). This is a well-documented critical study of multinational business activities.

G. W. Bell (ed.), *Global Companies: The Political Economy of World Business* (New Jersey: Prentice-Hall, 1975).

P. J. Buckley and M. Casson, *The Future of the Multinational Enterprise* (London: Macmillan, 1976).

J. H. Dunning (ed.), *The Multinational Enterprise* (London: Allen & Unwin, 1971).
A collection of some of the leading articles in this field.

H. G. Johnson, *Technology and Economic Interdependence* (London: Macmillan, 1975), chaps 4 and 5.
A spirited defence of MNCs as agents of economic development.

G. Paquet (ed.), *Multinational Firm and Nation State* (London: Collier-Macmillan, 1972).

G. L. Reuber *et al.*, *Private Foreign Investment in Development* (London: Oxford University Press, 1973).
This study, sponsored by OECD, provides one of the most comprehensive surveys of the effects of foreign direct

investment on economic development.

K. P. Sauvant and F. G. Lavipour, *Controlling Multinational Enterprises* (London: Wilton House Publications, 1976).

A collection of some recent articles and documents dealing with national and international attempts to regulate the activities of MNCs. It contains a fairly extensive bibliography.

United Nations, *Multinational Corporation in World Development* (New York: Dept of Economics and Social Affairs, 1974).

This U.N. report is a very useful and informative reference book for the general reader.

CHAPTER 7

Technology, Human Resources and International Competition

7.1 Labour Skills and Comparative Advantage

It is never an easy task for economists to remind policy-makers of the relevance of the principle of comparative cost or comparative advantage. It is not always understood and, when it is, it is rarely adopted without reservations. This principle – a triumph of economic logic – rationalises the mutual beneficiality of free international trade regardless of country sizes or degrees of affluence. The principle is regarded as being of fundamental importance in connection with the major issues in international economic relations, e.g. trade preferences for poor countries, multilateral trade negotiations, adjustment assistance policies and, of course, the continuing national arguments over protectionism versus liberal trade policies. But to give the principle concrete form, to make it operational, it has to be incorporated in a theory which explains the source of comparative advantage. The fact is, however, that economists have developed a bewildering variety of theories to explain the determinants of international specialisation and trade in manufactured goods. Considering these seemingly competing hypotheses of the sources of comparative advantage and the actual pattern of trade in manufactures it appears that comparative advantage in any given country can arise from relative capital or skill abundance, higher labour productivity or technological superiority. The variety of theories adds to our understanding of the forces underlying international competition, but gives rise to a certain ambiguity in the analysis or discussion of commercial policy matters. The purpose of this chapter is to survey recent theoretical and empirical analyses of the pattern of international trade and to assess the relative importance of the factors determining international industrial competition in the modern world.

Until very recently the Heckscher—Ohlin theory[1] was widely regarded as affording a complete and satisfactory explanation of the sources of comparative advantage and hence of the observed pattern of trade. The empirical prediction of the standard Heckscher—Ohlin theorem is that patterns of international trade can be explained mainly by differences in the relative endowment of countries with capital and labour. The original theorising by Ohlin recognised not only three basic factors of production considered in neo-classical writings – land (or natural resources), labour and capital – but also varying *qualities* of the first two of these factors. However, as the theory has been developed and refined in the hands of Samuelson and others it became conventional to work with two factors of uniform quality – labour and capital – both in theoretical analyses and empirical work. In contrast to the Ricardian theory that comparative cost differences between countries existed because the production function for a given commodity varied from one country to another and the extent of variation differed for the two commodities, the standard H—O theorem assumes that the production function for a given commodity is the same irrespective of the country of production, in the sense of identical capital–labour (K/L) ratios; although, of course, they vary from commodity to commodity. This factor-intensity difference in the production functions for different commodities, combined with differences in the factor endowments of countries, accounts for international differences in comparative costs of production. Given these assumptions and relations the conclusion emerges that countries possessing relatively more capital than labour would tend to have a comparative advantage and therefore to specialise in the production and export of commodities requiring much capital and little labour. Countries with abundant labour supplies and little access to capital would find it advantageous to concentrate on the production of items requiring relatively large amounts of labour.

The simplified H—O theorem as outlined above held great

sway among trade theorists until 1953 when the latter were forced to reckon with the now-famous 'Leontief Paradox'.[2] In the first major empirical test of the H—O hypothesis Leontief found that the manufacture of U.S. exports required a higher proportion of labour to capital than the manufacture of import-competing goods. Given that the United States is the most capital-abundant country in the world the H—O theory predicts quite unambiguously that the United States would export capital-intensive goods and import labour-intensive ones — hence the paradoxical nature of Leontief's findings.

Subsequently, Leontief-type tests were applied in experiments to determine the factor-intensity ratios of other countries' exports and imports. But since in about half of the studies undertaken theoretical predictions were at variance with the empirical results, confidence in the two-factor H—O theory was badly shaken.

The 'Leontief Paradox' therefore led to a re-examination of the assumptions of the theory, especially the non-reversibility of factor intensities in production. But the most relevant development for the purpose of this chapter stemmed from a suggestion of Leontief himself that American labour is sufficiently superior in quality to foreign labour for the United States to be a labour-abundant country. This suggestion Leontief throws out as a reconciliation of his empirical findings with the conventional theory. It was treated with some scepticism at the time. Yet, as it turned out, the notion of labour-quality differences proved to be extremely fruitful in the empirical approach to trade structure and patterns. Leontief made use of it in his second report on the structure of U.S. foreign trade. Here he incorporated a breakdown of labour inputs by major skill and occupational groups which enabled him to show that American exports were relatively more skill-intensive than American imports.

This was the breakthrough for the new approach to the analysis of trade structure that explicitly takes into account the education—skill characteristics of the labour force. This approach received considerable theoretical and empirical backing from the writings of researchers in the field of human capital theory. These writers focused attention on the role of expenditures on education and training, improvements in health and research, etc., in raising the quality of human capital and the continuing returns in the future that these outlays yield. It was no longer possible to speak of 'labour' in trade theory, as elsewhere as a single undifferentiated mass to be reckoned simply in terms of man-years. People invest in themselves (with varying degrees of public assistance) through education and training to acquire skills and competences that lead to returns in terms of income differential for various levels and types of skills in a process analogous to that of physical-capital formation. Skill, in fact, can be considered as a form of capital, since training is fundamentally a production process of an investment good: the skilled man. In coming to grips with economic facts trade theorists had to reckon with the fact that labour embodies human capital, that superior skills are acquired by the labour force through investment of resources, and the implications of this for the traditional concepts of 'factor abundance' and 'factor intensity'. For Leontief-type tests of the H–O theorem this implies that allowance must be made for the human capital element in factor-intensity comparisons if the explanatory variables are to be properly specified.

For instance, with reference to Leontief's second more detailed findings that U.S. exports were more skill-intensive than U.S. competing imports the computation of the capital value of the skilled-labour inputs in the exporting and import-competing industries should have been added to the physical capital employed to arrive at a more accurate measure of the relative intensities of the trade involved.[3] Similarly, the factor endowments of the United States would have to be correspondingly adjusted. In this way the empirical findings for the United States might be satisfactorily reconciled with the Heckscher–Ohlin hypothesis. Peter Kenen attempted to do just that on the basis of some rough calculations towards the end of an important article on 'Nature, Capital and Trade' (1965).[4] His estimates are based on the now generally recognised notion that different amounts of skilled labour in the production process result from different amounts of investment in human capital, so that the higher wages of skilled labour are properly regarded as returns to capital. The value of the capital embodied in the labour force depends on the amount by which the skilled worker's income exceeds that of an unskilled worker's, and can be capitalised at a suitable rate of interest. Computing the present discounted value of the human capital represented by these skill differences at a 9 per cent rate of return Kenen adds the direct and indirect human capital requirements to the physical-capital requirements and finds that U.S. exports become more capital-intensive in this wider sense than do import replacements. The result is even more striking when human capital (at the 9 per cent rate of return) is deflated by an index of consumer prices; it completely reverses the factor intensities thrown up by Leontief's method – thus resolving the Leontief Paradox.

The next step in developing the skill-differences approach to the analysis of trade patterns was taken by Donald Keesing.[5] Pursuing Kenen's hypothesis that the United States will have a competitive advantage in industries where there is much investment in human capital – skill-intensive industries – Keesing proceeded to test this hypothesis by a variant of the Leontief method. He does not use figures of investment in human capital, but concentrates on the skill-requirements of manufacturing industry (i.e. excluding natural resource-intensive industries) with a view to ascertaining whether the U.S. advantage lies in skill-intensive industries. The analysis is not cast in terms of K/L ratios, but S/U ratios (skilled over unskilled) in a treatment where different qualities of labour are regarded as separate productive factors.

The test itself involved the computation of the skill-content of exports and imports for the United States, seven European countries and Japan, using U.S. skill coefficients derived from Leontief's skill calculations. Keesing then ordered the countries by *direct* skill requirements (a departure from Leontief's procedure) in export production and, similarly, in import-competing production and showed a symmetrical ordering of countries. Those whose exports are most skill-intensive have the least skill-intensive imports. With this result Keesing concluded that skill availability is a major factor in the determination of trade patterns. The United States tends to export goods embodying large amounts of skill while importing goods embodying large amounts of unskilled labour. Keesing's findings lend support to the view that international differences in supplies of skills, reflecting different rates of investment in the labour force, affect trade patterns in a significant way. Countries well endowed with skills make the most of this advantage, while those less well endowed arrange their trade to conserve this scarce factor of production. Some doubts were raised against the use of U.S. skill coefficients to estimate the skill-intensity of other countries trade so Keesing reworked and updated his trade data, using skill coefficients from nine industrial countries to measure the skill-intensity of twenty-three countries' manufactured exports in 1965. International data on skills are based on job titles as recorded in national population censuses. Keesing was able to show: (*a*) strong similarities in industries' occupational mixes from one country to another, (*b*) high simple correlations (mean values above 0.98) between exports of the twenty-three countries and the skill coefficients from each of the nine leading industrial countries. The relative skill-intensity of other countries' trade flows as measured by U.S. skill coefficients are thus roughly duplicated when coefficients from any other leading industrial country are used instead.

In the last five years research on the role of human capital in foreign trade has progressed by leaps and bounds. From small beginnings conceived initially as an attempt at resolving the Leontief Paradox the thrust of recent research has established the robust character of explanatory variables having to do with human resources, skills and education. The point has been reached where the human capital account is now central in contemporary analyses of manufactured goods trade. To round off the discussion some of the more recent studies will now be examined. Of the five papers under review two were concerned with U.S. trade (Fareed, Baldwin),[6] the third was world-wide in coverage (Hufbauer)[7] and the remaining two applied the labour-skills extension of the H—O theorem to a developing country, Brazil (Lowinger, Tyler).[8]

Fareed estimated the U.S. human-capital stock in terms of the dollar costs of the accumulated investment flows that created it. With H standing for a human-capital component representing investment in the formal education of the labour force and L for labour, he tests the hypothesis that the average H/L ratio of 1947 U.S. exports was higher than that of its imports. Fareed found that, in 1947, U.S. exports required $2064 worth of *H*-stock per man, while import replacements called for $1846 worth. The ratio is therefore 1.118, so U.S. exports were more human-capital intensive than imports. U.S. trade for 1951 (a more normal trading year) was also examined. The *H*-intensity ratio of exports to import replacements fell to 1.071.

Next, again in regard to the United States, Baldwin made a study of the determinants of the commodity structure of that country's trade. His efforts at location and consolidation of data from many sources have shed new light on several competing hypotheses attempting to explain the commodity pattern of U.S. trade. An interesting feature of Baldwin's study is that here he marshalled a full array of industry characteristics as independent variables. These included capital–labour ratios, percentages of industries' labour forces in various skilled groups, costs of education of industries' labour forces, average years of education, average earnings of labour, degrees of concentration, extent of R & D activities, etc.

Using 1962 trade figures and 1958 industry characteristics he estimated the factor requirements per million dollars of U.S. exports and competitive imports. He also presented the results of his regression analysis relating the various economic characteristics of U.S. industries to the trade balances of those industries. Baldwin's results confirm the continued existence of the Leontief Paradox for the United States – the ratio of capital per man-year in import competing versus export production is 1.27. Here again, however, the hypothesis that export production involves higher skill requirements than import-competing production receives support as the figures for average earnings, average years of education and average costs of education indicate. The regression coefficients for the independent variables representing the proportions of scientists and engineers and other skilled workers in the industries' labour forces are statistically significant and have the theoretically correct signs in many cases. Baldwin also did a bilateral test involving U.S. trade *vis-à-vis* Western Europe, Japan, Canada and the developing countries. This did not materially alter the general picture that U.S. exports were more intensive in the use of human capital. For instance, although (looking at factor-content ratios) he found that U.S. exports to Western Europe and Japan were more physical-capital intensive than imports from these countries, the capital–labour variable did not show up as statistically significant in the multiple regression analysis. Other factors appeared more significant. In particular, the R & D variable and the variable representing the percentage of employees with thirteen or more years of education.

Gary Hufbauer tested several hypotheses concerning the international pattern of trade in manufactured goods, using a common set of data. He related the skill endowments of twenty-four countries to the skill content of their 1965 commodity trade (three-digit categories). Notwithstanding the imperfections inherent in such international comparisons the study obtained high rank correlation coefficients between national skill endowments and skill characteristics embodied in traded manufactured goods.

Turning to the Brazilian studies, these have been particularly welcome from the point of view of enhancing the generality of the human-capital account. Practically all the previous tests have been undertaken for developed countries. The experience of developing countries should also be instructive for the purpose of development planning; for if manufactured exports depend on skill endowments, then prevailing skill shortages or bottlenecks may constitute serious obstacles to the desired objective of export promotion of manufactured goods. Lowinger examined the commodity composition of Brazilian trade with the countries of North America and Western Europe. He first attempted to estimate the human and physical-capital endowment of Brazil relative to the above countries and to certain other Latin American countries. Brazil is shown to be deficient in both skilled labour and physical capital in relation to her trading partners in North America and Europe, although Brazilian deficiency is greater in skilled human resources. Lowinger next related two-digit SITC trade flows (1966) between Brazil and the industrial countries of North America and Europe to the characteristics of the traded commodities with respect to physical capital per man, skill ratios and wages per man. The results indicated that Brazilian imports from the industrial countries were intensive in both physical and human capital (especially significant were the two human-capital independent variables, the skill ratio and wages per man).

However, as regards Brazil's exports to the industrial countries the tests were inconclusive. No clear-cut pattern in her manufactured exports was observed. A different set of tests was proposed to analyse the competitive performance of Brazilian industry in order to reveal the comparative advantage basis of its trade pattern. Trade balance ratios, as well as ratios of gross imports to value of sales, imports to total imports were related to industry characteristics such as a skill index, horsepower per employee (proxy for physical-capital intensity) and value added per employee. The results strongly supported the human-capital approach. On the basis of these tests Brazil's comparative disadvantage is most pronounced in manufactured commodities requiring a great deal of skilled labour in their production.

The main findings of this study were corroborated by the more extensive analysis of the Brazilian case by Tyler. This author tested various hypotheses stemming from the labour-skills H–O theory, using an industrial cross-section of 1968 data. Skill requirements were estimated with both U.S. and Brazilian data. Four basic skill categories in twenty-one industries were identified from the 1960 Brazilian industrial census. The U.S. data were Keesing's skill coefficients for forty-six industries. The hypotheses subjected to testing included two of particular relevance in our context: (*a*) that Brazil's manufactured imports are more skill-intensive than its exports and (*b*) that Brazil's manufactured exports are less skill-intensive than those of more-developed industrial countries. Hypothesis (*a*) was confirmed. Both skill-intensity indices rank imports higher than exports. In addition, the average wage embodied in manufactured exports was 20.6 per cent lower than that for imports. However seemingly consistent with Lowinger's finding, hypothesis (*b*) was not confirmed. The composition of 1968 Brazilian manufactured *exports* implied an embodied skill-intensity similar to those of developed countries, ranking between France and Austria and above that of Belgium. If Brazil is relatively lacking in human capital why is it that it exports industrial products embodying relatively high levels of scarce skill resources? Tyler attempts to answer this question by further analysis. He shows that the paradoxical nature of Brazilian export composition lies partly in the market destination of her exports. For instance, although the embodied skill-intensity for the country's total manufactured exports was 0.340, the skill-intensity indices for exports to LAFTA on the one hand and developed countries on the other were 0.406 and 0.283 respectively. It was further suggested that the high natural resource content of some of Brazil's major exports, e.g. certain chemical products and factor market distortions help to explain the relatively high skill-(and capital-) intensity embodied in Brazil's exports of manufactures.

The results of the studies outlined above are collectively a tribute to the 'human investment revolution' in its impact on international trade theory. Paradoxes and unsettled issues have been partly resolved, and new avenues of approach explored. The notion of labour-quality differences and skill availabilities as pervasive influences on patterns of trade and location have led to the elaboration of a dynamic explanation running in terms of technological change as a source of trade in manufactures, especially among the developed countries. The tie-up comes from the fact that an innovating country would tend to have a higher proportion of its labour force in those occupations requiring extensive education and training, e.g. scientific, engineering and technical occupations.

7.2 Technology and Trade Patterns

Since the Second World War the world economy has undergone a widespread transformation in industrial structure and trading patterns under the stimulus of rapid progress in industrial and managerial technology and the ever-widening horizon of the corporation. As barriers to trade and capital movements were gradually dismantled, manufacturing and marketing became increasingly integrated among the industrialised countries. Firms in different countries find themselves exposed to new competition (and opportunities) in world markets. In this environment the only successful survivors are those who can innovate or adapt to the needs of on-going technologies. It is against this background that we must see the increasing interest among economists in technological change as a key determinant of international trade in manufactures. The limited number of empirical investigations, and the various new lines of enquiry opened up, strongly intimate that this is a rewarding approach to the study of international trade patterns. The idea that technological change has important consequences for international trade is, of course, not a new one. The classical and neo-classical economists, notably Mill and Edgeworth, looked at the influence of technology on trade, but almost exclusively they confined their analysis to its effects on the terms of trade. The origins of the modern concern with the issue can be traced to the discussions that went on shortly after the Second World War when there appeared to be a structural or chronic dollar shortage facing the European countries. One explanation for this phenomenon that carried conviction at the time was to the effect that technical change in one country would worsen the terms of trade and disrupt the balance of payments of her trading partners. It was natural, following the classical tradition, that the effects of differential technological growth should be traced largely through its effects on the terms of trade.

Subsequently the focus of analysis was broadened and generalised with a more ambitious perspective in view. Attempts were made to formulate hypotheses explaining trade that tended to discount the factor-proportions theory by showing that the ability to produce new products based on superior technology could constitute sources of comparative advantage additional or alternative to comparative advantage based on relative factor-abundance. As early as 1956, for instance, Irving Kravis put forward his 'availability' doctrine.[9] Kravis set out to explain the pattern of trade in manufactured goods by showing that the main determinant of this pattern is 'availability' or supply elasticities. Availability stems from three sources: (*a*) lack of natural resources, (*b*) technological progress and (*c*) product differentiation. The presence or absence of these factors or states of affairs make trade largely the exchange of goods which are available in one country but not in another; and Kravis suggests that it is in terms of these three factors that we must look for an explanation of the composition of U.S. exports. Technological progress and product differentiation work to confer a temporary monopoly on the innovating country; and where these are active elements in a country's industrial system Kravis indicates that we shall find that such a country's export industries will show higher rates of technical progress than the national average. Shortly thereafter Staffan Burenstam Linder produced his *Essay on Trade and Transformation*,[10] which attempted to discount the H—O theory by endeavouring to show the relationship between high income and trade in manufactures where technological change is more relevant than factor endowments. The composition of trade in manufactures is, he said, a function of many factors: technological superiority, managerial skills and economies of scale. Observing that the overwhelming proportion of trade in manufactures takes place between countries of similar economic structure Linder postulates that trade in manufactures is explained by similarity in demand patterns, i.e. he starts from the proposition that home demand is essential before a country can develop an exportable product. Technological innovation is more likely to flourish in those industries that cater for a sophisticated home market. The presence of a sufficiently large home market enables such expanding industries to reap economies of scale and gain competitive strength in foreign markets. The products of such industries are most easily exportable to countries where the composition of demand is about the same — which means countries with similar income levels.

While Kravis and Linder laid the foundations for the technological theory of trade it was left to writers such as Posner, Hirsch and Vernon to cast it in a genuinely dynamic framework.[11] The theory is essentially a disequilibrium theory of trade centring on the periodic emergence of new products as the result of scientific research (synthetic materials, semiconductors, computers, etc.), the export of such products by the innovating country, the elimination of this trade by imitative production elsewhere and the repeat of this cycle as new discoveries are made and new products developed. The theory therefore takes cognisance of the fact that in today's highly competitive markets, national and international, R & D activity is requisite to the survival of individual firms and national economies, and from investment in R & D new technologies are consciously generated. Trade based on such technologies is not only permanent, but growing fast in relative importance to trade in more traditional types of goods. A country's competitive viability depends on the rate at which it innovates (the number of new commodities or processes successfully developed and marketed per unit of time) and the speed with which it imitates foreign innovations. The theory emphasises that new technology is not universally available, i.e. production functions are not identical in all countries. Research-intensive firms in developed countries have a propensity to introduce new goods and improved (lower-cost) processes. Such firms will engage in innovations and develop products that are likely to be demanded locally, i.e. firms will respond to demands which are most familiar. The highly differentiated nature of a new product makes the demand relatively inelastic. These products will be typically those with high income elasticities of demand and they will be goods the production of which is saving in the use of labour in view of the relatively high cost of labour in innovating countries.

According to the product life cycle the history of a product can be divided into three stages: (i) new stage, (ii) mature or marketing stage and (iii) standardised or large-scale production stage. Of particular significance is the postulate that the different factors of production – skilled and unskilled labour, managerial ability and physical capital – are of varying relative importance in these phases. Thus at the initial stage when the firm has just invented a new product the firm will employ a large proportion of research scientists and engineers; inputs of physical capital will be small, i.e. employment costs of scientific and engineering personnel are likely to be a larger fraction of total expenditures in this phase than at later stages. At this early stage comparative advantage lies with the United States and certain other developed countries having a relative abundance of skilled labour. At the mature stage the problem becomes one of finding the best design and effective ways of selling the product. The proportion of research scientists will fall and inputs of management and ad-men will increase; but the firm will still not employ large numbers of unskilled workers. In contrast, by the time the product reaches the standardised stage the cheapest method of production will be to make large numbers. Technology will have become fairly stable, large production runs are possible; so this stage will call for relatively large inputs of semi-skilled and unskilled labour. Physical-capital intensity might also be high owing to large quantities of specialised mass-production equipment. At this stage human-capital needs will have diminished. The availability of cheap labour now becomes the decisive factor in determining location and trade patterns of the standardised product. Shifts in comparative advantage between countries occur as the product or process passes through the various stages of the cycle. The model also explains the considerable differences among countries in the composition of exports, imports and production in particular research-intensive industries. American exports and production will be heavily weighted with relatively new and advanced products and processes, while American imports will be mainly standardised products and processes. Japanese production and exports will consist mainly of the mass-produced, standardised varieties. European production and exports will fall somewhere in between. The factors determining a country's balance of trade in the new product or process are identified by the model. Although learning economies postpone the day, once the technology diffuses abroad and countries with lower wage rates and skilled manpower begin producing the product, the United States soon loses its comparative advantage. In order to maintain a favourable balance of trade that country must continually introduce new and better products and processes. Finally, it is of interest to note the interrelationship between trade and factor movements (specifically in the form of foreign direct investment) revealed by this new approach. This is especially apparent in the Vernon version, which is explicitly a theory of trade and investment. This theory envisages the gradual international transfer of production of new products. Firms in other industrialised countries may, by their own research or imitation, emulate the innovator at an early stage of the product cycle. The innovator may also accelerate the cycle by overseas direct investment or licensing. Two considerations are important in prompting such a transfer. First, as the product becomes more standardised and producible by mass-production method, i.e. involving large proportions of semi-skilled and unskilled labour, minimisation of labour costs will become increasingly important to producers. Competition might also increase the elasticity of demand facing the producer and reinforce the tendency to seek out low-production-cost locations. The innovating firm then finds it cheaper to locate in countries with lower labour costs. Second, through direct investment, the leaders can retain monopolistic control over price and output by forestalling foreign imitation.

The role of technological factors in determining the commodity composition of trade in manufactured goods has been empirically investigated by several writers in the last decade. Louis T. Wells tested the theory against the data on consumer durables (refrigerators, washing-machines, vacuum cleaners, etc.).[12] The regressions he worked out confirmed the hypothesis that the United States will pioneer the invention of goods with high income elasticity of demand, and that U.S. exports of such goods will expand more rapidly than those of other products. Hirsch's study of the U.S. electronics industry also supported the product-cycle explanation of the pattern of trade in that industry. Research by Keesing, Gruber, Mehta and Vernon and Baldwin showed that a significant and positive relationship exists between U.S. export performance and the R & D intensity of U.S. industries. Lowinger[13] recently examined the technology factor and the export performance of U.S. manufacturing industry and found that U.S. comparative advantage is most pronounced in research-intensive industries. His results indicated that up to 73 per cent of the variance of U.S. industries' exports is explained by differences in research intensity. He concluded that U.S. competitive performance in international trade is largely determined by the country's ability to invest a comparatively high proportion of its resources in the development of new products and improved production processes. In an analysis of the structural characteristics of Canada's trade with the United States Harry Baumann found that the technology model provides the best explanation of the bilateral pattern of trade in manufactured goods.[14] The export and import propensity, as well as the net balance of trade of a sample of sixty-seven Canadian manufacturing industries, were regressed against variables measuring human capital, physical capital, natural resources and technological intensity of these industries. Canadian imports are highest in respect of products with technologically unique characteristics or features. This indicates that Canada's role in the international product cycle is primarily that of an imitator. Canada has a relatively low commitment to R & D and relies heavily on technological borrowing from the United States through direct investment and licensing.

It is becoming demonstrably clear that the physical-capital version of the H–O theory is inadequate in explaining actual trade patterns. Physical capital does not seem to be important in influencing the export/import pattern of developed countries. To a large extent, in so far as manufactured goods are concerned, these countries are engaged in intra-industry trade, i.e. specialisation in production and export of products having capital input requirements very similar to imported substitute products. The spread of multinational companies across countries has given the world economy a high degree of capital mobility (both financial capital and capital goods). Theoretically, we expect that high capital mobility would lead to a convergence of inter-country factor payments to capital. If this is the case then skills, technology and raw labour remain the only factors determining comparative advantage. As the product-cycle theory indicates, and experience bears out, a country's technological lead can quickly be dissipated by the efficient international dissemination of knowledge. As innovations spread from one industrial country to another shifts in comparative advantage present problems of adjustment and adaptation affecting growth prospects and standards of living in countries involved in technological trade. For instance, in the early 1970s the United States became uncomfortably aware of the steady erosion of its trading position in technology-intensive manufactured products – chemicals, electronic equipment, machinery and transport equipment. U.S. imports of such products grew twice as fast in the 1960s as exports. Protectionist measures were advocated in Congress, and the Administration proposed new measures to foster innovation in high-technology lines. Although the United States still enjoys a sizeable trade surplus in technology-intensive products, the rising trend of imports of such products reflects the closing of the technology gap with Europe and Japan. A 1970 OECD survey disclosed the fact that U.S. firms originated nearly two-thirds of the successful innovations since 1945. In the mid-1960s U.S. firms had the largest individual share — about one-third — of world exports in technologically advanced products; for instance, in 1964, the United States accounted for 60.5 per cent of industrial countries' exports of electronic capital goods and for 59.5 per cent of such countries' aircraft exports. The reduction in America's technological lead since that time clearly illustrates the diffusion process at work. MNCs speeded up the diffusion of American know-how. The United States became the largest exporter of patents and licensing knowledge. But equally important were the successful efforts by European countries and Japan in building up their technological capabilities through increased spending on R & D. Japanese spending on R & D, for instance, increased more than sixfold in the 1960s. By contrast, the pace of American R & D expenditure slackened during the same period (to 5 per cent annually, compared with a rate of 12.6 per cent from 1953 to 1964).

7.3 Indices of Competitiveness

One aspect of the theory and measurement of general equilibrium trade flows that is worthy of consideration concerns the measures commonly used as indicators of comparative advantage. In recent empirical work a bewildering variety of measures have been employed to indicate what various writers loosely call 'competitive strength', 'trade competitive power' or more simply, 'competitiveness'. What is referred to, of course, by such talk is comparative advantage or the lack of it in particular commodity groups with reference to a given country. But it is not always clear how these terms relate to the same basic notion of comparative advantage. In this section we shall briefly discuss the choice of measures and their limitations.

Empirical tests of trade theories are concerned with the analysis of trade flows by major industrial categories and their relation to country attributes. In the case of the H–O theory the commodity composition and quantity of a country's exports (imports) are explained by its relative factor endowments. Differences in factor endowments between countries would give rise to inter-country differences in comparative costs; these cost differences would, in turn, be reflected in comparative price differences. Price variables, however, are in general excluded in most empirical work designed to test trade theories. In contrast to the analysis of competitiveness at the micro or partial equilibrium level, in the context of the pure theory of trade, we use, in effect, cross-section equilibrium functions. In a general equilibrium setting prices are endogenous and merely adjust to equate supply and demand. This point can be clarified by considering demand and supply schedules as follows:

$$q^D = f\ (p,\ D_1,\ D_2,\ \ldots,\ D_n)$$

$$q^S = g\ (p,\ S_1,\ S_2,\ \ldots,\ S_m).$$

This indicates that the quantity demanded (q^D) depends on the price (p) and a set of demand factors D_i, and that supply behaves similarly. We can solve (or obtain the reduced form of) these equations for the market clearing quantity:

$$q = q^S = q^D = h\ (D_1,\ D_2,\ \ldots,\ D_n,\ S_1,\ S_2,\ \ldots,\ S_m).$$

That is, the observed quantity depends on the demand and supply functions, but not the price variable. What is ordinarily done in empirical work is to assume that abundant exports are the necessary and sufficient indicator of low prices. Thus, given the commodity characteristics (e.g. capital-intensive) and the national attributes (e.g. relative abundance of physical capital) abundant exports of capital-intensive commodities from a capital-rich country would be indicative of comparative advantage. And the country's 'competitiveness' can be gauged by the extent to which this is true.

Accordingly, country exports by commodity groups feature prominently as the dependent variable which is related to country attributes (such as relative abundance of physical capital, relative abundance of professional workers and highly trained labour, etc.) in analyses of trade patterns. The focus tends to be on exports, primarily because exports are typically less distorted by domestic policies than imports. However, as an indicator of comparative advantage exports on their own suffer from at least three disadvantages. First, tariffs and quotas severely limit certain international markets, e.g. cotton textiles. Textile commodities are consequently understated in the exports of countries with textile advantages. Second, a country's own import restrictions affect its export composition by drawing resources directly and indirectly from the export industries. If a skill-intensive activity enjoys high domestic protection, this will retard those exports also dependent on skills. Third, if one believes that comparative advantage can and should guide policy-making, then trade theory should generally focus on net trade flows rather than just exports, since the policy variables with which we usually are concerned are framed in net terms, e.g. balance-of-trade or net employment effects of trade policy changes.

The various indices of comparative advantage commonly resorted to can be grouped into three categories:

E_1 – A ratio of exports to total sales in each industry.

E_2 – The excess of exports over imports as a percentage of sales. Or, sometimes, the difference between exports and imports divided by the sum of exports and imports. This is a net trade balance index.

E_3 – An export share index.

All of these indices are calculated for individual industry outputs and exports.

Index E_1 can hardly be thought of as a measure of a country's comparative advantage in any given industry (or industries). Such a measure, after all, is not only a function of the competitive position of the country's industry; it also reflects, among other things, (a) the structure of demand abroad as compared with the country in question and (b) the effects of impediments to free international trade. Substantial differences in demand structures between the country and its trading partners might be reflected in the export/sales ratio of industries without any underlying comparative cost differences. Also, neglecting the import side of the trade balance would ordinarily bias the results of tests due to inter-industry differences in tariffs and transport costs. One might neverthe-less want to use this index for purposes other than testing a trade theory – for instance, to explore the relative significance for a country's export pattern of individual influences, e.g. tariffs. Including foreign and domestic tariffs (along with scale variables, etc.) as independent variables in multiple regression analysis can be used to confirm the hypothesis that the higher are foreign and domestic tariffs then, other things being equal, the smaller should industry exports be as a percentage of domestic sales. The high foreign tariff reduces the possibilities of the country's manufacturers achieving economies of scale through exports and of their being able to export even if optimum scale were developed within the domestic market. The high domestic tariff may militate against cost reduction and effective competition in world markets by providing a protected market for domestic producers.

Index E_2 goes a little way in the direction of allowing for the effects of demand differences and trading frictions. But theoretical analysis leads one to suspect comparisons based on the net trade balance of individual industry outputs. For if there are more goods than factors then the output mix is indeterminate in general equilibrium.

Index E_3 is a measure which relates the export performance of a country's industry to the export performance of the same industry localised in prospective competitor countries. The 'normalising' variable becomes the total industry exports of all the countries concerned, rather than the total sales of the particular country's industry. For instance, Keesing in some of his work took U.S. exports in each industry as a percentage of the exports of the OECD countries in the industry. Normalis-ing a country's exports by total exports for each industry satisfies the objections to indices E_1 and E_2 to a large extent, because all these countries (i.e. the developed countries) face similar inter-industry differences in trade barriers. The distor-tion due to international divergences in demand structure is moderated by focusing on the competitive ability of a country's industry *vis-à-vis* other countries of roughly similar levels of development. The export share, although not a measure of traditional comparative advantage, is thus a fairly reliable indicator of export performance. It provides a method of ranking industries which does not depend on their absolute or relative importance in the domestic economy as would using simply the value of exports or export minus imports, or on their importance in total world trade as would exports divided by domestic output.

Some investigators use a simple trade balance index $\frac{X}{M}$ (exports divided by imports). This is at least no worse, and a good deal better, than some other variants of comparative advantage. It takes account of demand difference and transport frictions. Where these are holding down exports, therefore, they may also be expected to hold down imports. It also provides an acceptable indicator if one is restricted to using only one country's trade data. None of these measures is ideal, though. Different results are sometimes produced depending on which measures are used. In some respects an ideal measure in regard to competitiveness would be a country's exports as a percentage of world consumption or production and in regard to net trade flows imports should be included and measured as a percentage of the country's consumption or production. In addition it would help if we could use free-trade exports and imports; but, of course, it is difficult to measure the degree of protection both at home and abroad. To a large extent finding credible measures of comparative advantage is part and parcel of the general problem of trying to identify empirical counterparts to the theoretical constructs of trade theory.

If one is interested not so much in the comparative-advantage basis of a country's trade (in connection with abstract models of international trade), but in the country's international competitiveness as understood by business and international money managers then one must look at trends in the country's unit labour costs relative to labour costs trends in other competitor countries. A comparison of unit labour costs offers the best available indicator of a country's performance in international trade in manufactured goods. Such trends are useful not only in analysing trade flows, but also for forecasting trade balances. Unit labour costs – the costs of labour per unit of manufacturing output – are determined by hourly compensation and labour productivity. Labour compensation includes gross pay, fringe benefits and other production costs attributable to labour such as social security contributions, payroll taxes, etc. Labour productivity is the relationship between hours worked and the physical volume of output. A persistent rise in a country's index of unit labour costs relative to the indices of foreign competitors indicates a weakening of its competitive position. In the short run, of course, rises in labour costs can be absorbed by reduced profit margins or sales at distress prices which fail to cover fixed costs so as to maintain output and employment. But in the long run such increases in unit labour costs must be reflected in higher export prices which eventually erode a country's competitive advantage in export markets. Under the old system of fixed exchange rates inter-country shifts in unit labour costs were reflected in strengthening or weakening of trade balances. In the present regime of managed floating, cost changes exert their influence on currency values, although not as promptly as under a system of truly floating exchange rates.

Further Reading

R. Findlay, *Trade and Specialisation* (Harmondsworth: Penguin Books, 1970) chaps 3–5. Highly recommended elementary treatment of the H–O and technological gap theories of trade.

H. G. Johnson, *Comparative Cost and Commercial Policy Theory for a Developing World Economy*, Wiksell Lectures, 1968 (Stockholm: Almqvist & Wiksell, 1968).

J. F. Morrall III, *Human Capital Technology and the Role of the United States in International Trade* (Tallahassee, Fla: University of Florida Press, 1972).

B. Södersten, op. cit., chaps 4–7.
A clear textbook exposition of the H–O theory and the earlier empirical work on the Leontief Paradox.

R. M. Stern, 'Testing Trade Theories', in P. B. Kenen (ed.), *International Trade and Finance: Frontiers for Research* (Cambridge: Cambridge University Press, 1975) pp. 3–49.

R. Vernon (ed.), *The Technology Factor in International Trade*, NBER (New York: Columbia University Press, 1970).

Notes and References

Introduction

1. K. N. Waltz, 'The Myth of Interdependence', in C. P. Kindleberger (ed.), *The International Corporation* (Cambridge, Mass.: M.I.T. Press, 1970) pp. 205–23. For comments on the Waltz definition see R. Rosecrance and A. Stein, 'Interdependence: Myth or Reality', *World Politics*, vol. 26, no. 1 (Oct 1973) 1–27.

1. Multilateral Trade Negotiations

1. Whereas in the early 1960s organised labour in the United States gave enthusiastic support to the Trade Expansion Act 1962 which initiated the Kennedy Round, in the early 1970s the AFL–CIO pushed for passage of the protectionist Burke–Hartke Bill. The proposed legislation would have imposed universal quotas on American imports reducing them by 40 per cent and drastically restricting the export of U.S. capital. Together with the mushrooming of protectionism in other countries, this would have brought international trade and investment to a low ebb.

2. See W. M. Corden, *The Theory of Protection* (Oxford: Clarendon Press, 1971), for a review of the main criticisms of the theory of effective protection. This work also contains a comprehensive bibliography on theoretical and measurement problems.

3. U. Hiemenz and K. von Rabenau, 'Effective Protection of German Industry', in W. M. Corden and G. Fels (eds), *Public Assistance to Industry* (London: Macmillan, 1976) pp. 7–45.

4. N. S. Fieleke, 'The Pattern of US Tariffs: The Myth and the Reality', *New England Economic Review* (July/Aug 1974) 15–18.

5. N. Oulton, 'Effective Protection of British Industry', in W. M. Corden and G. Fels (eds), op. cit. pp. 46–90.

6. See G. K. Helleiner, 'Transnational Enterprises and the New Political Economy of US Trade Policy', *Oxford Economic Papers*, vol. 29, no. 1 (Mar 1977) 102–16.

7. There are exceptions; for instance, see C. P. Kindleberger, 'Group Behaviour and International Trade', *Journal of Political Economy*, vol. 59, no. 1 (Feb 1951) 30–47, where he compared the responses of different European countries to the fall in grain prices in the late nineteenth century. More recently, he has presented a detailed interpretation of the free trade movement in nineteenth century Europe in terms of State solicitude of the interests of powerful groups – 'The Rise of Free Trade in Western Europe 1820–1875', *The Journal of Economic History*, vol. 35, no. 1 (Mar 1975) 20–55.

8. See S. Guisinger and D. Schydlowsky, 'The Empirical Relationship between Nominal and Effective Rates of Protection', in H. Grubel and H. Johnson (eds), *Effective Tariff Protection* (Geneva: GATT, 1971), and B. I. Cohen, 'The Use of Effective Tariffs', *Journal of Political Economy*, vol. 79 (Jan/Feb 1971) 128–41.

9. See S. P. Magee, 'The Welfare Effects of Restrictions on U.S. Trade', *Brookings Papers on Economic Activity*, vol. 3 (1972) pp. 645–707.

10. For an up-to-date analysis of the taxation of export profits see G. C. Hufbauer 'The Taxation of Export Profits', *National Tax Journal*, vol. 28, no. 1 (Mar 1975) 43–59.

11. This is ironic since it was the use of agricultural export subsidies by the United States that provided the E.E.C. with a precedent and an argument to build up its variable levy system.

12. For a short statement of the E.E.C.'s position on agricultural trade with the United States, see M. Lardinois's speech to the Conference on Community – American agricultural relations in Monterey, California, 24 August 1976, reported in *European Community*, no. 7 (Sept 1976) 3–4. For a fuller account of the agricultural trade dispute between the E.E.C. and the United States see *E.E.C. Trade Relations with*

the USA in Agricultural Products (Centre for Agricultural Studies, Wye College, Ashford, Kent, 1977).

2. Trade and Debt Problems of the Third World

1. T. K. Morrison, 'Manufactured Exports and Protection in Developing Countries: A Cross-Country Analysis', *Economic Development and Cultural Change*, vol. 25, no. 1 (Oct 1976) 151–8.

2. See J. N. Bhagwati and A. O. Krueger, 'Exchange Control, Liberalisation and Economic Development', *American Economic Review*, vol. 63, no. 2 (May 1973) 419–27.

3. Australia was, in fact, the first country to implement a preference scheme for which she obtained a waiver from GATT in 1966. But the Australian scheme only applied to a rather small range of goods in favour of a limited group of LDCs.

4. U. Hiemenz and K. von Rabenau, op. cit. p. 28.

5. Since 1 January 1974 the volume of duty-free trade is based on 1971 trade figures, rather than those of 1968.

6. Z. Iqbal, 'The Generalised System of Preferences Examined', *Finance and Development*, vol. 12, no. 3 (Sept 1975) 34–9.

7. Tracy Murray was one of the first writers to show the quite limited benefits of the GSP when the institutional constraints are incorporated in the analysis. See T. Murray, 'Preferential Tariffs for the LDCs', *Southern Economic Journal*, vol. 40, no. 1 (July 1973) 235–46.

8. See R. E. Baldwin and T. Murray, 'MFN Tariff Reductions and Developing Country Trade Benefits Under the GSP', *Economic Journal*, vol. 87 (Mar 1977) table 4, p. 41.

9. Among several commentaries on the NIEO the following are noteworthy: H. G. Johnson, 'World Inflation, the Developing Countries and "An Integrated Programme for Commodities"', *Banca Nazionale del Lavoro Quarterly Review*, no. 119 (Dec 1976) 309–35; M. E. Kreinin and J. M. Finger, 'A Critical Survey of the New International Economic Order', *Journal of World Trade Law*, vol. 10, no. 6 (Nov/Dec 1976) 493–512; C. H. Kirkpatrick and F. I. Nixson, 'UNCTAD IV

and the New International Economic Order', *The Three Banks Review*, no. 112 (Dec 1976) 30–49.

10. The Conference on International Economic Co-operation (called on French initiative) met in Paris for the first time in December 1975. It brought together 27 participants representing industrial countries, OPEC nations and the LDCs. The Conference's task is to reach broad agreement on policy issues relevant to LDCs trade and development that are currently under debate in larger forums (e.g. UNCTAD, GATT, the Development Committee of the World Bank, etc.). Meetings were suspended in December 1976, but were resumed early in 1977.

11.   A. I. MacBean, *Export Instability and Economic Development* (Cambridge, Mass.: Harvard University Press, 1966).

12.   G. F. Erb and S. Schiavo-Campo, 'Export Instability, Level of Development and Economic Size of Less Developed Countries', *Bulletin of the Oxford University Institute of Economics and Statistics* (Nov 1969) 263–83.

13.   MacBean, op. cit. chap 4; P. B. Kenen and C. S. Voivodas, 'Export Instability and Economic Growth', *Kyklos*, vol. 25, fasc. 4 (1972); O. Knudsen and A. Parnes, *Trade Instability and Economic Development* (Lexington, Mass.: Lexington Books, 1975) chap 6.

14.   E. M. Brook and E. R. Grilli, *Commodity Price Stabilization and the Developing World*, World Bank Staff Working Paper, 1977, summarised in *Finance and Development*, vol. 14, no. 1 (Mar 1977) 8–11.

15.   See World Development Movement, *A New Deal for the Poor* (London: 1977).

16.   Speech by M. Cheysson, E.E.C. Commissioner for Development, to London Europe Society, London, April 1977.

17.   See T. M. Klein, 'The External Debt Situation of Developing Countries', *Finance and Development*, vol. 13, no. 4 (Dec 1976) 21–5.

18.   An attempt to put LDC debt into perspective is R. Z. Aliber, 'Living with Developing Country Debt', *Lloyds Bank Review*, vol. 126 (Oct 1977) 34–44. See also D. C. Beek, 'Commercial Bank Lending to the Developing Countries',

Federal Reserve Bank of New York *Quarterly Review*, vol. 2 (Summer 1977) 1–8.

3. East–West Trade

1. The standard text on COMECON covering the first fifteen years of its existence is M. Kaser, *Comecon*, 2nd rev. ed. (London: Oxford University Press; R.I.I.A., 1967). A more recent account is H. W. Shaefer, *Comecon and the Politics of Integration* (New York: Praeger, 1972).

2. For an empirical investigation of the effects of U.S. restrictions on American exports to COMECON see J. C. Brada and L. J. Wipf, 'The Impact of US Trade Controls on Exports to the Soviet Bloc', *Southern Economic Journal*, vol. 41, no. 1 (July 1974) 47–56.

3. See J. M. Hertzfeld, 'New Directions in East–West Trade', *Harvard Business Review*, vol. 55, no. 3 (May/June 1977) 96.

4. See A. Bergson, 'Towards a New Growth Model', *Problems of Communism*, vol. 22, no. 2 (Mar/Apr 1973) 1–9.

5. See *Morgan Guaranty Survey* (Sept 1972) p. 8.

6. See M. M. Tardos, 'Interactions Between Planned and Market Economies – Hungary', in M. Allingham and M. L. Burstein (eds), *Resource Allocation and Economic Policy* (London: Macmillan, 1976) p. 54.

7. See J. Wilczynski, *The Multinationals and East–West Relations* (London: Macmillan, 1976) p. 56.

8. See S. Rosefielde, 'Factor Proportions and Economic Rationality in Soviet International Trade 1955–68', *American Economic Review*, vol. 64, no. 4 (Sept 1974) 670–81.

9. In an empirical investigation of the foreign trade of E.E. countries (1960 and 1970) based on a trade-flow model developed by Linnemann, Adam Broner shows that E.E. countries' foreign trade participation does not exhibit any autarkic tendency. A. Broner, 'The Degree of Autarky in Centrally Planned Economies', *Kyklos*, vol. 29, fasc. 3 (1976) 478–94.

10. See A. Brown, P. Marer and E. Neuberger, 'Prospects for U.S.–East European Trade', *American Economic Review*,

vol. 64, no. 2 (May 1974) table 4, p. 304.

11. For an analysis of the background to the Complex Programme and the progress of COMECON integration see Z. M. Fallenbuchl, 'Comecon Integration', *Problems of Communism*, vol. 22 (Mar/Apr 1973) 25–39.

12. In addition to the adverse effects on Eastern long-term planning, Western inflationary trends and the oil crisis led to great difficulties in the management of E.E. economies. For a good summary of the effects these changes in external market conditions had on economic management in Hungary see M. M. Tardos, op. cit. pp. 52–60.

13. For an informed and up-to-date discussion of the impact of East–West trade on the prospects for economic integration in COMECON, and the argument that further integration is to be expected – to the detriment of East–West Trade, see A. Korbonski, 'Detente, East–West Trade, and the Future of Economic Integration in Eastern Europe', *World Politics*, vol. 28, no. 4 (July 1976) 568–89.

4. The Eurodollar Market, Short-term Capital Flows and Currency Crises

1. The Eurodollar market forms part of a wider external currency market, commonly known as the Eurocurrency market. Apart from dealing in dollar deposits, banks in the Eurocurrency market also accept and make loans in deutschmarks, Swiss francs, etc. However, we focus attention on dollar transactions as the dollar is by far the dominant Eurocurrency, accounting for more than 70 per cent of the outstanding net total of Eurocurrency deposits. What is distinctive of the Eurocurrency market as a whole is that banks deal in deposits denominated in currencies other than those of the country in which they are located. Thus, Euro-banks in Germany issue deposits denominated in dollars, Swiss francs – or, indeed, in any currency other than deutschmarks.

2. Of course, where organised markets in forward exchange exist, investors can normally arrange to buy forward cover to match the maturity of their foreign assets, thereby insuring themselves against unfavourable exchange-rate changes.

3. See M. J. Hamburger, 'The Demand for Money in an Open Economy: Germany and the United Kingdom', Federal Reserve Bank of New York, Research Paper no. 7405 (Apr 1974) mimeo, pp. 17–19.

4. Mundell's original contribution to the development of the theory of the 'optimum policy mix' in an open economy can be found in R. A. Mundell, *International Economics* (London: Macmillan, 1968). For a survey of the literature see M. von N. Whitman, *Policies for Internal and External Balance*, Special Papers in International Economics 9 (Princeton University, International Finance Section, Dec 1970).

5. The literature on the monetary approach to the balance of payments is expanding rapidly. Theoretical and empirical papers in this area have been collected in J. A. Frenkel and H. G. Johnson (eds) *The Monetary Approach to the Balance of Payments* (London: Allen & Unwin, 1970). For a short, simple exposition of the policy implications of the monetary approach see H. G. Johnson, 'The Monetary Approach to the Balance of Payments', *Journal of International Economics*, vol. 7 (1977) 251–68. This was one of the last articles written by the late Harry Johnson.

6. F. A. Lutz, 'International Payments and Monetary Policy in the World Today', Wiksell Lectures, 1961 (Stockholm: Almqvist & Wiksell, 1961) p. 37.

7. The debate on the question of credit creation in the Euromarket is an old one. It apparently started with an article by Geoffrey Bell, 'Credit Creation through Euro-dollars?', *The Banker*, vol. 114 (Aug 1964), in which he claimed that 'the market could, under certain conditions, act in the same manner as a domestic banking system and from a given flow of dollars from the United States, increase the total stock of world dollar liquidity by some multiple' (ibid. p. 494). Milton Friedman entered the fray in 1969 and argued in similar vein – that Eurobanks, like Chicago banks, are part of a fractional reserve banking system ('The Euro-dollar Market: Some First Principles', *Morgan Guaranty Survey* (Oct 1969)). Dr Fred Klopstock, of the New York Federal Reserve Bank consistently dissented from this interpretation and denied that there is a strict analogy between the Eurobank system and a domestic banking system. Primarily on account of the large 'leakages'

from the Eurobank system, he estimated a low Eurobank money multiplier – between 0.50 and 0.90. See F. H. Klopstock, 'The Euro-dollar Market: Some Unresolved Issues', *Essays in International Finance*, no. 65, (New Jersey: Princeton, 1968) 8. Although the lenders in the Euromarket are commercial banks, in reality, they operate as non-bank financial intermediaries, he maintained (F. H. Klopstock, 'Money Creation in the Euro-dollar Market', *Monthly Review*, Federal Reserve Bank of New York, vol. 52, no. 1 (Jan 1970) 12–15).

8. See J. Hewson and E. Sakakibara, 'The Euro-dollar Deposit Multiplier: A Portfolio Approach', *IMF Staff Papers*, vol. 21 (July 1974) 307–28.

9. The analysis is contained in *Monthly Economic Review*, First National City Bank (Feb 1976) 9–12.

'5. World Monetary Arrangements

1. But this clause was never invoked because the United States – the one country against which it might have been applied in the early years of the IMF – offset the dollar surplus with generous gifts and loans to Europe for post-war reconstruction.

2. For early comments on the reform measures and the proposed new Articles of Agreement, see E. M. Bernstein *et al.*, 'Reflections on Jamaica', *Essays in International Finance*, no. 115 (Apr 1976) (New Jersey: Princeton University Press). Also, T. de Vries, 'Amending the Fund's Charter: Reform or Patchwork?', *Banca Nazionale del Lavoro Quarterly Review*, no. 118 (Sept 1976) 272–83.

6. Multinational Corporations

1. This trade union pressure for measures to control imports and the export of jobs was particularly strong during the U.S. recession of 1969–70. American unions warned that U.S. multinationals' world-wide activity was turning the United States into an economy 'dominated by hamburger stands, motels, importers, international banks, and similar activities

without the broad base of diverse and varied industries and production'. Quotation from AFL – CIO, 'An American Trade Union View of International Trade and Investment', in U.S. Senate Committee on Finance, *Multinational Corporations* (Washington, D.C.: U.S. Government Printing Office, 1973) p. 80.

2. J.-J. Servan-Schreiber, *The American Challenge* (Harmondsworth: Penguin 1969). Originally published in French as *Le Défi Americain* (Paris: Denoël, 1967).

3. *The Impact of Multinational Corporations on Development and on International Relations* (United Nations, 1974) (4 vols, E. 74 II A. 5, A. 6, A. 7 and A. 8). See also the background report by the U.N. Department of Economic and Social Affairs Secretariat, *Multinational Corporations in World Development* (1973).

4. R. Vernon, *Sovereignty at Bay* (New York: Basic Books, 1971).

5. J. K. Galbraith, *Economics and the Public Purpose* (Harmondsworth: Penguin Books, 1975) chap 17.

6. For a good interpretation of the main features of Japanese multinational business activity in the light of existing theories, see Terutomo Ozawa, 'Peculiarities of Japan's Multinationalism: Facts and Theories', *Banca Nazionale del Lavoro Quarterly Review*, no. 115 (Dec 1975) 404–26.

7. For a detailed discussion of the development by MNCs of 'export platforms' in LDCs and the system of international sub-contracting see G. K. Helleiner, 'Manufactured Exports from Less-Developed Countries and Multinational Firms', *Economic Journal*, vol. 83 (Mar 1973) 21–47.

8. See D. R. Weigel, 'Multinational Approaches to Multinational Corporations', *Finance and Development*, vol. 11, no. 3 (Sept 1974) 29.

9. S. Lall, 'Multinationals and Development: A New Look', *National Westminster Bank Review Quarterly Review* (Feb 1975) 56–64 provides a short statement of some of the problems involved in multinational activity in LDCs. For a fuller discussion of the issues, see chap. 6 in R. J. Barnet and R. E. Müller, *Global Reach: The Power of the Multinational Corporation* (London: Cape, 1975).

10. See S. A. Morley and G. W. Smith, 'The Choice of

Technology: Multinational Firms in Brazil', *Economic Development and Cultural Change*, vol. 25, no. 2 (Jan 1977) 239–64.

11. W. A. Yeoman, 'Selection of Production Processes for the Manufacturing Subsidiaries of U.S.-Based Multinational Corporations', DBA thesis, Harvard Business School, 1968.

12. See G. L. Reuber, *Private Foreign Investment in Development* (Oxford: Oxford University Press, 1973), and L. T. Wells Jr, 'Economic Man and Engineering Man: Choice of Technology in a Low Wage Country', *Public Policy*, vol. 21, no. 3 (1973) 319–42.

13. Details are to be found in B. I. Cohen, 'Comparative Behaviour of Foreign and Domestic Export Firms in a Developing Country', *Review of Economics and Statistics*, vol. 55, no. 2 (May 1973) 190–7.

14. See R. H. Mason, 'Some Observations on the Choice of Technology by Multinational Firms in Developing Countries', *Review of Economics and Statistics*, vol. LV (Aug 1973) 349–55.

15. B. Cohen, op. cit.

16. R. D. Morgenstern and R. E. Müller, 'Multinational Versus Local Corporations in LDCs: An Econometric Analysis of Export Performance in Latin America', *Southern Economic Journal*, vol. 42, no. 3 (Jan 1976) 399–406.

17. The evidence is contained in C. V. Vaitsos, 'Interfilliate Charges by Transnational Corporations and Intercountry Income Distribution', Ph.D thesis, Harvard University, June 1972, p. 42. Vaitsos's work has become more accessible with the publication of his book, *Intercountry Income: Distribution and Transnational Enterprises* (London: Oxford University Press, 1974). Transfer pricing in general is investigated in S. Lall, 'Transfer pricing by Multinational Manufacturing Firms', *Bulletin of the Oxford University Institute of Economics and Statistics*, vol. 35, no. 3 (Aug 1973).

18. R. Müller and R. D. Morgenstern, 'Multinational Corporations and Balance of Payments Impacts in LDCs: An Econometric Analysis of Export Pricing Behaviour', *Kyklos*, vol. 27, fasc. 2 (1974) 317.

19. A tax haven is a place or country where foreigners may receive income or own assets without paying high rates of tax upon them. Examples of tax havens are the Bahamas, Bermuda, Hong Kong, Liberia, the New Hebrides and Panama.

20. U.S. Department of Commerce, *Survey of Current Business* (Sept 1973).

21. See Vaitsos, 'Interfilliate Charges . . .', op. cit., note 17, above.

22. D. B. Furnish, 'The Andean Common Market's Common Regime for Foreign Investment', in K. P. Sauvant and F. G. Lavipour (eds), *Controlling Multinational Enterprises* (London: Wilton House Publications, 1976) chap. 9, pp. 181–93.

23. See *Trade in Primary Commodities: Conflict or Co-operation?* (Washington, D.C.: The Brookings Institution, 1974) p. 39.

24. See J. M. Stopford and L. T. Wells, *Managing the Multinational Enterprise* (New York: Basic Books, 1972).

25. On the idea of a GATT-type framework for regulating MNC activity see the discussions in D. Wallace Jr (ed.), *International Control of Investment: The Düsseldorf Conference on Multinational Corporations* (New York: Praeger, 1974). Participants at this 1973 Conference felt that GATT-type rules were unnecessary in the case of developed countries and impracticable in relation to LDCs.

7. Technology, Human Resources and International Competition

1. See B. Södersten, *International Economics,* chap. 4, for a lucid statement of the H–O theory. For a recent comprehensive survey of trade theories and the results of empirical testing see R. M. Stern, 'Testing Trade Theories', in P. B. Kenen (ed.), *International Trade and Finance: Frontiers for Research* (Cambridge: Cambridge University Press, 1975) pp. 3–49.

2. Leontief's original article is reprinted in W. W. Leontief, *Input-Output Economics* (London: Oxford University Press, 1966) chap. 5, pp. 68–99. See Sodersten, op. cit. chap. 7, on the Paradox.

3. Although intuitively appealing, this procedure of combining estimates of human and physical capital to determine the capital–labour ratio in trade-oriented production rests on the assumption that human and physical capital are perfect

substitutes; but it is obvious that they are not, at least in the short run.

4. P. B. Kenen, 'Nature, Capital and Trade', *Journal of Political Economy*, vol. 73, no. 5 (1965) 437–60.

5. D. B. Keesing, 'Labor Skills and International Trade: Evaluating Many Trade Flows with a Single Measuring Device', *Review of Economics and Statistics*, vol. 47 (1965) 287–94.

6. A. E. Fareed, 'Formal Schooling and the Human-Capital Intensity of American Foreign Trade: A Cost Approach', *Economic Journal*, vol. 82, no. 326 (June 1972) 629–40. R. E. Baldwin, 'Determinants of the Commodity Structure of U.S. Trade', *American Economic Review*, vol. 61, no. 1(Mar 1971) 126–46.

7. G. C. Hufbauer, 'The Impact of National Characteristics and Technology on the Commodity Composition of Trade in Manufactured Goods' in R. Vernon (ed.), *The Technology Factor in International Trade*, NBER (New York: Columbia University Press, 1970) pp. 145–272.

8. T. C. Lowinger, 'The Neo-Factor Proportions Theory of International Trade: An Empirical Investigation', *American Economic Review*, vol. 61, no. 4 (Sept 1971) 675–81. W. G. Tyler, 'Trade in Manufactures and Labor Skill Content: The Brazilian Case', *Economia Internazionale*, vol. 25, no. 2 (May 1972) 314–34.

9. I. B. Kravis, ' "Availability" and other Influences on the Commodity Composition of Trade', *Journal of Political Economy*, vol. 64 (Apr 1956) 143–55.

10. S. B. Linder, *An Essay on Trade and Transformation* (Stockholm: Almqvist & Wiksell, 1961).

11. See Hufbauer, op. cit. pp. 184–93.

12. L. T. Wells Jr, 'Test of a Product Cycle Model of International Trade: U.S. Exports of Consumer Durables', *Quarterly Journal of Economics*, vol. 82, no. 1 (Feb 1969) 152–62.

13. T. C. Lowinger, 'The Technology Factor and the Export Performance of U.S. Manufacturing Industries', *Economic Inquiry*, vol. 13 (June 1975) 221–36.

14. H. Baumann, 'Structural Characteristics of Canada's Pattern of Trade', *Canadian Journal of Economics*, vol. 9, no. 3 (Apr 1976) 408–24.

Index